I0149786

Where Science and Religion Meet

By

William Scott Palmer

ISBN:978-1-63923-208-6

Printed: May 2022

Cover Art By: Amit Paul

Published and Distributed By:
Lushena Books
607 Country Club Drive, Unit E
Bensenville, IL 60106
www.lushenabooksinc.com/books

ISBN: 978-1-63923-208-6

Table of Contents

CHAPTER I

The moon shines in my body, but my blind eyes cannot see it:
The moon is within me, and so is the sun.
The unstruck drum of Eternity is sounded within me;
but my deaf ears cannot hear it.
Kabir.

Deep in every one of us there is a passion of desire to understand, just as there is of desire to enjoy and of desire to be somehow or other 'in the right.' I say deep in us, because we are in the habit either of burying these desires beneath a pretence of satisfying them or else of diverting our attention from them and thus letting them sink out of sight. So we live our life in the pursuit of other ends than those likely to be reached through understanding and rapture and righteousness. We falsify ourselves and our desires; yet unless we ruin the life within us they persist, waiting their hour.

There are moments when it becomes almost impossible for any man who has seen something of the marvel of every-day affairs to believe that he might spend time in vain if he were to try to convince his next-door neighbour that there was anything hard to understand about the crooking of a finger. Yet that is his experience when he tries. Just because every man who has a healthy finger in a healthy body and a healthy mind can and does crook it, there is nothing to wonder at. The whole affair is plain; it is familiar, happens every day. Familiarity lulls to sleep both the desire for understanding, and the sense of not understanding.

Consequently there is little that should provoke surprise on our part in the fact that not one man in (say) ten thousand is consciously puzzled by any of the deeper problems of life, not one in (say) a hundred thousand has his imagination either stirred or stunned by the green blades of the corn, the leaves of the tree, the grass in his fields or the sheep and cows that are eating it. There is nothing new about all this, nothing strange; it is familiar—therefore it is understood or there is nothing that calls for understanding. Yet in these green blades and leaves is the junction-point between the living and the not-living, between the plant and animal on the one hand and what we call 'inert matter' on the other, between the radiant energy of the sun and ourselves. And we do not understand, nobody understands, how that junction-point works. It is called chlorophyll; it is found in little living bodies called chloroplasts; and it is wonderful 'beyond all whooping'. Yet we do not even whoop. We do not get even thus far. We are not surprised, we are not enraptured. The thing is at once both too familiar and too obscure for us.

We cannot do away with the familiarity; but at least, as reasonable beings possessed of that passion of desire which is a cry of the spirit within us and which we so often do our utmost to suppress, it will be well for us to make an attempt to find out how and even why this green stuff of the plant is so highly distinguished among the wonders of the world.

But first let us ask ourselves a searching and pertinent question—let us ask ourselves what it means to be alive. A man is alive, but so are the cells of his own blood, so is the grass in the fields, so are the small jellies we call amoebae and the still smaller rods and specks we call bacteria and 'germs.' Can we say anything about life that will at once fit these and distinguish them from all else that does not live, accepting for the moment the distinction between living and not-living that we ordinarily make?

There are several things that we may say about them. For example, they grow. But a crystal grows and so does a heap of sand. There are, then, different ways of growing. The sand heap grows when the wind scatters particles of sand over it or the sea drives them; or the river, or a small boy with a barrow, deposits them. It grows by mere addition. The crystal grows without any such aid and in a different way. If you want to see an alum-crystal grow you must offer it more alum, dissolved; you must offer it its own material and it will then grow without other help. It will grow by what we may call formative accretion. On the other hand the grass and the corn and the trees grow neither by mere addition nor by formative accretion, but by converting, assimilating and incorporating nitrogen, carbon, and so on, compounded either by their own effort or by the micro-organisms of the soil. They are magicians, these live creatures. And of all their magic the magic of their green leaves is chief in our eyes. For it takes the carbonic acid of the air, a stable compound of one atom of carbon with two of oxygen, and tears it to pieces, using for that enormous work the radiant energy of the sun. This carbon, now potent with the potency of the sun, is then united with other elements to make sugars that nourish the tissues of the plant. In these sugars power is stored as it is stored in an explosive like dynamite or trinitrotoluol. But in the plant, power is under strict control; it is liberated by degrees as it is wanted and is replaced as it is used; it is controlled, used, replaced in a discriminating, selective and determining way. The ability to make use of physical power, within a body, in this discriminating, selective and determining way and thus to grow is (among other things) what is meant by being alive.

The chemist in his laboratory can make explosives, chemical compounds that will easily break down and in breaking down will liberate, for good or ill, great power. He makes nitroglycerin and trinitrotoluol. He can also make very elaborate and more stable compounds than a plant makes, for instance, indigo or madder-red, though for such as these he does not usually begin like the plant with chemical elements; he begins half way—with lesser compounds, ready made—and thus, or even sometimes by building up from the bottom, from elements, like the plant, he makes what are known as 'organic' substances of many sorts and uses. Is it possible that he will ever make that organic substance protoplasm, the life-jelly of living things? He has not done so yet. Suppose he did, suppose he went on from making indigo to make the indigo-maker itself. There is nothing of a chemical kind in the indigo-plant which his laboratory does not contain; there are just the carbon, nitrogen, oxygen, salts and the rest, with which he deals so successfully elsewhere. He has all the materials to hand. Why should he not make its living stuff? Again, suppose he did, for perhaps he will. What then? Will he have made life, as well as built up the material substance of a living thing? That is a question of questions.

We know life here only in association with its jelly. What is the character of that association? Granted that life depends on the jelly, in what way does it depend? If we can answer these questions we may know how to answer the one about the chemist's making or not making life, if and when he makes the jelly.

There are different ways of being dependent, as there are different ways of growing. The steam depends on the boiler and the boiler-fire. In this case the dependence is one of being *produced*. The boiler and its fire produce the steam. So we say, in the ordinary way of speaking of such things. Again—when I press the trigger of a rifle the bullet is shot out. I have only pressed the trigger; you can hardly say I have produced the bullet. What I have done is to release an explosive power that drives the bullet. That is another kind of dependence, dependence on the *release* of power. There may be still, there certainly have been, men who would tell you that life is produced by protoplasm as steam is produced by the boiler, or that it is released from a chemical compound by some chemical or physical trigger action. They might, once they did in large numbers, say that consciousness is produced by or released from the brain, and that this must be so because it depends upon the brain.

These two assertions, one about life and the other about consciousness, stand or fall together; and we can begin to see that they may be made to fall, as soon as we see that there is a third kind of dependence to be considered besides the dependence of the bullet and the steam. There is the dependence of light in a room on the existence of a window. Without window no light in that room; with window as much light as window permits to pass. There is a dependence of *transmission*, and transmission may occur in many wide and fundamentally differing ways. At a stroke you see the whole question and series of questions take on a new aspect. If the chemist makes life-jelly he may have made not something to produce or to release but something to transmit life. He may doubtless have imitated what there is good reason to think must have taken place on the earth's surface long ago and may indeed be taking place now; but in doing this he may only have made a material substance capable of allowing spiritually potent life to be manifest in it and to endow it with a share in promoting the purposes of life. He may have made for the peculiar potency of life a door of entrance to a house, or rather, since this house is not passive, to a body in which it and the body will be distinguishable as a living being, an example of life and matter living and at work together. Why not? The supposition of some such dependence of the superior power of life upon a body seems quite as reasonable, even at no more than a first glance, as the other suppositions made by men who do not acknowledge the specific character of life. And it accords far better with both knowledge and experience, when these are taken at their widest and their most profound. The other suppositions accord only with chosen parts of knowledge and chosen bits cut out of experience—the parts and bits cut out and chosen by the man who restricts himself to the specialism and the very right and proper superficiality of certain sciences. Even there they accord but ill, because in their inception they trespass beyond the borders of all science.

Living creatures are the subject of the mere biologist's merely scientific inquiry—not life. When a biologist, speaking as biologist, tries to tell us both *that* life is and *what* it is, he is philosophizing. Life is in fact an ultra-scientific problem. We have to call in philosophy before we can even state the problem. And when either the biologist or the physicist or the chemist talks of life as a mode of physical or chemical energy, or as a product of things, he is playing at philosophy, not soberly working at his science. The biologist shall teach us about living creatures, the physicist and the chemist about physical and chemical things and powers; but the philosopher must help us in our enquiry about life. And this, not because a man shall not be permitted to transgress boundaries we lay down, but because his chosen methods preclude his walking safely except within boundaries they themselves build up. Of every specialist this is true. We must transcend specialism if we would have 'all things, like the stars in heaven,' shed 'their light upon one another.'

CHAPTER II
Time hath endless rarities, and shows of all varieties;
which reveals old things in heaven, makes new
discoveries in earth, and even earth itself a discovery.
Sir Thomas Browne.

The green leaf of the tree, the blade of the wheat that gives me bread—I look at them and tell myself, as many a man has told himself before, that if I could read their secrets I should know, as from the 'flower in the crannied wall,' 'what God and man is.' So I might, but only as far as their secrets go. If I could read my own I should go farther and know more. I am man and hold far greater secrets in being man. And I have the inestimable advantage of being inside myself, of being alive, besides looking on at living, of both growing and watching growth. There is no other live creature on earth who can possibly tell me as much as I can tell myself about what it means to be alive. And if the blade of wheat is wonderful beyond words, what am I?

Think of it: I have a history; indeed I am a history, I am time alive, time that accumulates and lasts. I have a past that is not past, because it is at work in my present and is writing its indelible signature on my future. There is no least action in my past that has not left its impress on me, made me different from what I should have been without it, and therefore will make my future different too. My whole history is alive, active and changing in my actions and my change. The history of my forefathers, too, is alive in me and in my character and powers. I have an inheritance from their living; I am as and what I am, in part because they were as and what they were. But I have power and I use it to create myself and recreate my inheritance through an impetus transmitted to me in the transmission to me of my life. Therefore every moment of my life is a unique and original moment of a unique and original history, mine and mine alone, never to be repeated, never to be wholly predicted, even by me. The evolutionist philosophy tells me that I endure, I *last*, and that all my changes and experiences endure, last, in and with me, changing in themselves and among themselves as though they were alive to influence and interpenetrate each other. Indeed they are alive in me and in my life or they could not endure. They would pass like the stages in the height of a sand heap as it grows, as the little heap it was is merged and lost in the larger heap it is. They would be lost as the flowing tide is lost when the ebb succeeds it. Such changes are mere successions, displacements and replacements; they are not history. They enter history only in sharing that of the universe which itself endures, lasts, and within which they are parts.

I, on the other hand, have a life of my own; I am a maker, shaper, creator. I am a master-worker and freeman in a world of relative necessity. Yet my wonderful living body, through which I do my work, depends for its support on the green blades of grass and corn and the green leaves of the trees. Further—every cell of the millions and millions in my body is like the amoeba and the cells of the plant in consisting of protoplasm. Further still—I began my own life as a speck of protoplasm, and if I could trace all the steps of my pedigree to the first display of life on earth, from which I am sure I am descended, I should (I dare to say) find another protoplasmic speck with which every one of the cells of the vast cellular republic whereby and wherein I live is in historical continuity. Bodily I am immensely complicated; I am a congeries and a commonwealth of cells. But the first cell was also complicated although it was but one. Nothing that lives is simple, no, not even if we carry the idea of life far beyond the arbitrary boundaries commonly set to it now. There is unplumbed mystery in the conjunction of two atoms of hydrogen with one of oxygen to make a third and different substance, water; there is unplumbed mystery in every element and every happening of the world. But some mysterious things are scientifically more complex than others, and among the most complex is this thing, protoplasm. Yet it seems that before life could be manifest in the world the molecular complexity of protoplasm must have been attained. By storing power in building up the atoms of the chemical elements from electrons, and making that power useful by the union of atoms in molecules; then, by a further delicate union between molecules (much after the fashion of widely branching, but only slightly tenacious, magnets) forming larger and ever larger groups, a condition of such plasticity of matter and ready discharge and restoring of power has been attained as makes it fit for the rank of a recognized life. The grouped and complicated molecules, each charged with power, are set as with a double-acting hair-trigger, so ready are they to let go energy in heat and work as these are wanted; so ready also for their rebuilding in the peculiar power of the life with which they are imbued.

There are examples of highly complex union to be seen in the chemist's laboratory and elsewhere which are never called living matter. The chemist speaks of some of them as colloids (we should naturally call many of these jellies, or gums) and he calls protoplasm a colloid too. They have remarkable properties, and the new bio-chemist thinks he may some day make that elaborate colloid with more remarkable properties, which we know as protoplasm. He thinks also that we do ill to confine the first production of life-jellies to the age of steaming seas and cloud-shadowed lagoons, before the Pre-Cambrian geologic times. He tells us that in his opinion it may always be going on and always have gone on since the earth was cool enough to permit of it. He thinks that if all the living creatures we are aware of were swept out of the world to-day there would still be living stuff remaining on it of which we are ignorant now; and that in the course of millenniums this would people it once more.

The beginnings of the life-jelly must be so small as to be far out of the reach of our microscopes and every other tool we can bring to bear, as yet, he says. And there, doubtless, he is right.

Let us suppose that he is right, too, in his main contention. Let us look at inorganic matter with a new eye, seeing in its evolutionary change the forerunner of greater change and greater evolution, the preparer of the narrow pathway by which life approaches to its display, and at last enters on possession of a body that in union with it shall be the germ of lives to come—enters the realm of physical forces and the relative necessity of material things, where and by use of those forces it will subdue necessity to the purposes of freedom. This indeed seems to be the manner and purposing of life as it extends from the single cell to the assemblage of cells that constitutes my body. There is continuity from first to last; and yet the differences between me and the primitive jelly-speck are even more striking than the resemblances. Students of the cell itself and students of my body as merely composed of cells are, naturally, cytologists, histologists, physiologists, embryologists, and the like. But unless there are others, unless students of psychology, ethics, aesthetics, social science, history, and many more, bring their minds to bear on me, I am studied to little sense and in small part. I am obliged to regard myself as not only physical but psychical; I seek after, and sometimes find, goodness and truth and beauty. I admire, I hate or love. I am a hero or a criminal, or both. I sin. In the advance of life from the minute and primitive colloid lump to me amazing things have happened. When I see life making its humble appearance by that speck of jelly, I must in my mind's eye connect it with what I am, and see there in its almost inchoate wonders the promise of myself. And still I must look behind even that first living thing and consider matter as well as life; for the physical potency of that thing was long of building up; and this physical potency has its place in me. The material pathway of life is the pathway of my powers, and it stretches far back into cosmic happenings smaller or (it depends how you look at these high matters and what you see in them) greater still.

We have no need to stretch imagination unaided; we may watch changes going on which indicate or, maybe, reproduce, stages in the creation of our own world and of its very elements. There are stars in which material elements are being either made or destroyed; it is hard for us to say which. In the constellation Argo there are two suns—furnaces of immeasurable heat—in which hydrogen, the lightest and simplest of our elements, is either being born or disintegrated before our eyes. There are other stars where hydrogen is in the same state as that in which we know it here, and more complex elements (for the elements of the chemist are in reality complex; they are only elements for him, because he cannot disintegrate them) are being born or, again, are being destroyed. There are stars in all stages up to the stage of our own sun and beyond, in age and powers; and there are elements of many degrees of complexity. In the series of those stars there is a series of changes which, taken together, mark for us either an ascent of matter from the immaterial, or a descent towards it. There is iron in its very infancy to be seen in some—proto-iron we call it—which we are able to produce ourselves by exposing ordinary iron to the intense heat of the electric vacuum spark and there disrupting it into a simpler mode which the spectroscope detects as it detects it in a star. We are entitled to say that in these changes material elements declare themselves to be things that somewhere and somehow are born and grow, whether in any one stage that we watch they are moving in one direction or another, from birth or down towards death. Indeed the most probable thing is that in the solar furnace-fires both movements are going on together; elements are being born and elements annulled. They have an origin, these elements. Some scientific men suggest to us that they issue from the universal ether that fills the interstellar spaces and the spaces of the stars themselves, of our own bodies, of all things in all worlds. Here the first stones of the pathway on which life travels may have (in their belief) been shaped. And neither chemist nor physicist can even guess at anything beyond. We stop here, as men of science only. It is at a place full of marvels that we are arrested. This ether is so marvellous that some rash men have deemed it competent to replace God. They have asked what need we have of any other God. And, truly, if the creations of worlds that are no more than physical were all a God was needed for, this amazing source of worlds would seem, not so unreasonably, to be enough. Whether the ether is immaterial or not, we might say the same. There are those who hold that it is the first and finest of the elements of matter. For men who know most about it, it is no kind of matter. But its power and fertility remain, however this may be; it is held to be the medium of communication everywhere, between small and great, distant and near; and the womb of the worlds. Undoubtedly it may serve the pseudo-physicist-philosopher in place of God, while he is no more than that.

The pathway for life has been traced back and back to the utmost of the regressive journey of science. We have seen (perhaps) the first stones being fashioned in the fires of the suns; at least we may believe that in some such place and way they have been and are being fashioned. We know—radium has shown us and the proto-iron—how chemical elements can be disintegrated and brought down to lower states of material complexity. In radio-active matter there is more than a hint that they may be brought lower still, returned to the fecund mother from which they came, restored, let us say, to the ether.

We may have learnt—that depends on our prepossessions—we may have learnt in studying this regress to see in what the chemist calls the 'affinity' of one element for another, and in its 'valency' (that is, its ability to grip one or another and even several to itself and take part in building up compounds), a likeness or a congruity with living stuff. And we have seen a living thing as compounded physically of the compounds of the chemist, though not, as yet, compounded by him. Unless our prepossessions form in us irrational prejudice we may gladly follow the clue science puts in our hands, and confess a continuous advance in order upon order of nature from the womb of the ether to ourselves.

CHAPTER III

There the Eternal Fountain is playing its endless
life-streams of birth and death.
Kabir.

We have followed the physicist and the chemist to the
farthest point they have reached in their research. They
cannot show us anything beyond, and we, unsatisfied, must
look elsewhere. The problems of life remain. We ourselves
stand on the great pathway, its continuous road of rising
orders, and from our place of vantage we contemplate the
first living thing. A profound discrepancy, or what seems
like one, stares us in the face, the discrepancy between our
mastery over things and our self-conscious, self-creative
abilities on the one hand, and, on the other, that first humble
yet awe-inspiring revelation by elements generated, perhaps,
within a white-hot star. Science has nothing to do with
meanings and purposes and values in our lives or with our
concern for them. Indeed it has nothing to do, in strictness,
with meanings and purposes and values anywhere. This is
the business of philosophy and of all ordinary men.

We have learnt a lesson as we followed the men of science
from step to step, and heard nature respond to their questions
with intelligible answers. We have learnt that, so far as it has
been examined, the universe, like ourselves, is rational and
has a history. It moves, changes, grows; it is real and its
history is real too. And though science is not concerned with
its meaning, we are. We hold fast to our science, but we care
for more than science. We cannot help it, for we are aware
of meaning in ourselves; as the man of science is when he is
not being only scientific. We are aware too of purpose and
of values; we are aware of making and shaping and creating;
we know what it is to choose and direct, to arrange and
rearrange, to produce novelty. Both sides of our knowledge
and our caring, the scientific side and the personal side, make

a difficulty for us in regard to the philosophers with whom we shall put ourselves to school. Our chosen teachers must reckon with life as we know and possess it in ourselves; but they must reckon too with every word of the scientific man. Nothing less will content us now. The philosophers we shall follow must not be playing a game among themselves, using thoughts like pieces on a board, to be moved according to rules they have laid down. Neither must they resolve the great drama of real things and real history into a phantasmagoria of mind; nor try to educe mind, consciousness, the spiritual activities of man, from the interplay of parts of a material machine. In our view both the material and the spiritual are real. It is for the philosopher, so we think, to show us the real relation between them. To do him justice, the philosopher has been thoroughly aroused of late years to the importance of reckoning with science. Consequently he draws to his side thinking ordinary men as they have perhaps never been drawn before, except when Socrates at Athenian banquets and in Athenian streets 'made himself a fool that others by his folly might be made wise.' We have no difficulty now in finding a philosopher, indeed many philosophers, to our mind. Philosophy is alive, sitting at our banquets, walking in our streets, even writing books that ordinary men, living each his own extraordinary life, can read. We are able to call in our philosopher, then, as we have called in the bio-chemist, knowing him to be one who reckons to the full with science, that he may tell us what he can and will concerning life and living.

A philosopher of that mind and reckoning has presented us with a picture in which we see life coming (may be from very far, coming, we may think, although concealed, by the material pathway from the ether that science has revealed to us) as an enormous impetus which finds the first of its advantages that are discernible by us, in that colloid assembly of compounded, complicated, delicately-strung, hair-trigger-hung elements, the protoplasmic stuff. We plainly see a new beginning which, in philosophic truth, is a continuance in new manners upon this earth of that which has no beginning; we see a living thing which lives because an impulsive and propulsive life, not material but spiritual, has raised material elements from the rank of dust, and has found a means of using material powers to purposes and ends. And this philosopher tells us that from its marvellous but humble first appearing in matter life advances, not like the trickle of a single stream, but like the bursting forth of a potent, spreading fountain whose waters part in a thousand directions to make a thousand streams, each purposive, each at first seeking, but many of them unsuccessfully, to fulfil some part of the purpose of the whole. And in regard to this frequent unsuccess, we find the philosopher borne out by the palaeontologist, whose 'general picture ... of the evolution of the animal kingdom is accordingly that of an immense number of ... lives which evolve parallel to one another, and without coalescing, throughout longer or shorter geological times,' each of which 'culminates sooner or later in mutations of great size and highly specialized characters, which become extinct and leave no descendants.' At the heart of life, as in the philosophic mirror we watch its advance, there seems one guiding and supreme purpose, which is manifest in the continuous effort 'to engraft on the necessity of physical forces the largest possible amount of indetermination,' that is, of freedom in choice. But this purpose is evidently very hard to fulfil, and as we see, often fails of being fulfilled.

We may in mind and imagination walk in company with these teachers of ours; we may see the stages of the past of living creatures marked out in the geological strata, learning thus how life has grown from less to more, how its divergent streams have turned this way or that, and how some have been frustrate, as in the giant saurians and labyrinthodonts.

We may learn too from the biologist that in our own day others (for instance perhaps those in the elephant and the ostrich and the whale) are in like manner drawing near to frustration by that impressive wearing out and perishing of a race, which is so clearly illustrated in the geological record. We discover that when impulsive life, seeking a free way, finds advance only through an excessive increase in the size of some creature, that creature's fate is sealed, and that manner of advance is barred. Size extending much beyond a certain range normal in the particular kind of animal is (perhaps in consequence of purely mechanical influences) to all the main intents and purposes of life no better than a blind alley. A like impulse, finding its outlet in the elaboration of nervous apparatus ranging from an all but indiscoverable structure to that definite and complex yet indefinitely mobile organ of an indefinitely extending choice—that living instrument for overcoming mechanism, that 'veritable reservoir of indetermination'—the human brain, finds there and there alone a road to great and full success. Yet it finds a road to minor and circumscribed successes in the lives of plants and animals which, interacting together, become of immeasurable value for the whole realm of life and the well-being of its citizens—for that realm of interlacing purposes and ends, where partial failure is so often converted to a new and a remoter triumph.

It seems as though in many, indeed in most instances, a life current, instead of driving on towards either greater freedom or complete arrest, met with a resistance able to constrain it, as it were, into eddies, wherein it circles as creatures living out either in a relative independence or in a parasitic state (sometimes of primary development, at others of degradation from a higher mode) their restricted lives. They are being fulfilled according to their restricted wants; they are needing no more of life than they have, and therefore seek no further than they are. And they have their co-operative value in the whole. These are the minor, yet many of them—and that in spite of dangers and pain and death—the delightful, successes of life. Everywhere upon this earth now, it seems, except in man, we may justly picture the life-currents as either coming to an end or circling round and round in some such eddy, at most curving out a little way to change a little in shape, to form new varieties within a species or, rarely, new species within a genus. There is in lower animals than ourselves, and in the plants, a certain contentment, on which tired men have sometimes been known to look with envy. The realm of nature is well served by servants such as these, and natural delights, in spite of natural pains, are won. But not all that life can do and be is represented in those finished forms. In the plants it seems to be asleep. There the protoplasmic stuff has built a wall about its soft body, the casing of cellulose behind which it sleeps, working in sleep, in great measure cut off from the varied stimulus and many-tongued summons, the resistances and opportunities, of an outer world. And some of the animals that are now extinct owe their extinction, not to their gigantic size, but to their having sought safety rather than adventure, and imprisoned themselves in their mechanical armour of defence. They too were in their measure cut off from the stir and help and moving oppositions of associated lives. In truth and in regard to the supreme purpose manifested in life, all the non-human creatures of the earth have, within themselves and for themselves, in one fashion or another barred its advance; although very many of them are furthering its purposes, indeed giving them indispensable support, elsewhere. Those which have not been extinguished and still maintain their place in the world are too complete, too well-adapted to a satisfying but narrow sphere, for progress to a wider. Life is not bearing them on; their nervous organ, that structure of inter-related cells by which they use their world, selecting and determining this or that, has not like ours capacity for indefinite change. Theirs is exactly fitted for their narrow use of it, and they and it are constrained together.

When we look at man through the eyes of the philosopher we see life clearly as a *spiritual* impulse, an impulse of a higher order than the animal, at least as much higher as that is than the material, and ever driving on. Man is not content; he is not fulfilled. He is fully awake; and he is not only conserving his long past but peering into the distances of his future. His brain is flexible, and able to provide a multitude of new structural arrangements; it is therefore an instrument of such choice as gives him leave to shape his future. And it is an active instrument; it brings to him through extending perception a field for his own spiritual activities that stretches out to match them, and enables him to become a ruler among circumstances. It allows him to worship beauty and even to create it; and to seek and worship truth; to adore goodness and be good. It permits desire to grow and the spirit within him to reach limit after limit, using each limit as an opportunity for further growth. All this the brain of man allows and promotes; and on this earth his brain alone. There is nowhere so magnificent and marvellous a bodily organ; for in it and by means of it physical things and physical laws are subdued to the purposes and ends of a free enduring creation.

CHAPTER IV
Listen to the moaning of the pine, at whose roots
thy hut is fastened.
Kabir.

The divergent streams of that primaeval fountain of life as they spread out upon the earth, in the earth, in the air, in, under and upon the waters, have given to it the endless variety of its creatures. In this variety, and of those streams, there are three and no more than three main currents; there are three directions and grouped characters and qualities of life. Each of these in its turn branches into minor streams and differences of creatures. The main currents are those of the plants, the insects, and the vertebrate animals.

We have seen that one function of the life of plants gives to the whole world of living creatures access to the energy of the sun. Yet as regards intelligence and conscious relation with other creatures the plant may be said to be asleep; it carries on its vital functions and builds up its manifold and admirable structures, working as though in sleep. Its whole activity, varied though it be, is like that of a dreamer. Confined within a wall of cellulose, the plant-cell works out its life as though, for its awareness, no other creature lived.

With the insect-world we enter on a widely differing scene. There, in the highest insects, we discover what may well rouse a salutary discontent with ourselves. The life-current which finds its eddying termination in the wasps and bees and ants has one, and that its chief, character pointing to grave but happily not irremediable deficiency in most of us, if not to some extent in all. The wasp seems to know other creatures' life, to understand it sympathetically, to touch and feel it from within, in a manner that to us is marvellous. Life manifests through this little winged thing a power we call instinct, perfected for certain uses to a degree not attained outside the insect-world. There are wasps which sting caterpillars with admirable though not invariable precision in their nerve-centres, so that they go on living but cannot move, and thus are made to serve as living larders for the wasp-grubs. Observers have found that different wasps, seeking different kinds of prey, sting three times, nine times, in three or nine centres, according to the number in the body of their selected victim, and that the Scolia stings the larvae of the rose-beetle in one point only, just where the motor-ganglia are concentrated. Other observers have noticed some failures and occasional irregularities. But listen (it may be once more and after many times) to this well-known story, the story of the Sitaris, if you want to see what life can do in a fashion for which the intellectual work of man offers in his experience no parallel. This tiny beetle lays its eggs in the doorway of the underground passages dug by a certain bee, the Anthophora. When an egg is hatched the grub awaits an opportunity to spring upon the male bee as it comes out. You may deceive it with a substitute, and no doubt it often is deceived without your help. Nevertheless, if not thus deceived it clings to the bee until the nuptial flight occurs, when it seizes some chance of shifting from the male to the female. Now clinging to the female, it waits until the bee-eggs are as usual laid upon honey. Then it leaps again, this time upon an egg which serves it at first as a raft on the honey. By degrees it eats up the egg; then uses as its raft the empty shell. It changes, undergoes a metamorphosis, and becomes able both to float and feed on honey, where it remains until it changes for the last time into the perfect insect, a Sitaris ready in its turn to set going this amazing cycle of life. It is a life that seems to involve knowledge of things which, by any knowing such as our intellectual experience provides, could not be known. Untaught, unaided, without previous experiment, the creature displays what looks like, but cannot be, true forethought, as well as ingenuity and adaptive skill; what looks like, but cannot be, a continued adjustment of reflectively chosen means to reflectively recognized ends. There can be no question but that all this, under such conditions, would be beyond the reach of our intellectual powers, and beyond our reflective thought. We may justly say that it is beyond the reach of any powers that are merely of reflective thought. Not thus does intellect carry on its conceptual work. It analyses and reflects, it separates, compares, and puts together. That is not the way of the grub of Sitaris, neither is it the way of the solitary wasp. There appears to be for these and for others of their tribe, in 'perceptual consciousness,' some mysterious sympathy between the life of the creature using and the life of the creature used, akin to that sympathy of digestive secretions with digestible food by means of which our bodies are nourished, or the process by which the cell becomes the organized and completed creature. There seem to be also motor-habits stored up by repetition in forbears, which facilitate the active expression of this sympathy. When the wasp stings the nerve-centres of the caterpillar as accurately, as on the whole he does, it seems to us as though in the mere presence together of wasp and caterpillar two congruous activities, not two beings, met—the wasp-activity perceiving rather than thinking about the caterpillar-activity, perceiving it and attacking it through certain established instrumental means as though entering into a familiar relation to it. You might be inclined to say that the sting of the wasp picks out the nervous ganglia of the caterpillar as a magnet picks out fragments of steel from the dust. Instinct no doubt means perceiving in sympathetic relation, and has more than a mere likeness to reflex actions in the body. Like these it may find its bodily support in a motor tradition, borne from reproductive germ to reproductive germ, as a structural record of bodily movements ingrained by the incessant repetition of certain actions through many continuous generations. But unlike these it may work with and for the intellect in all its grades.

We may well desire a sympathetic relation with other life, a perceptive understanding keener, quicker, more direct, more inclusive and more penetrating. And let us hasten to assure ourselves that we may attain what we seek, though in ways very different from the insect's, and for ends very different too. No life-current in any creature is of one character alone; none but has in it, in some proportion or another and with this or that degree of emphasis, all characters. The intuitive character and power of life in perceptive experience and perceptive consciousness, which though highly emphasized in some creatures becomes narrowed to their instinct, is not the exclusive prerogative of any one kind, even of the insects, though within their narrow bounds they have carried it almost to inerrancy of use; any more than reflective thought is the exclusive prerogative of man, though he has carried it farther and wider and deeper than any other creature of the earth. The problem for us is in great part one of emphasis and proportion. We have cultivated our reflective thinking more than our perceptive awareness, our conceptual more than our intuitive power. Because thought exercised upon external things has given us what we most wanted in the external world, and is giving us more and more, we have over-emphasized it. We have strained unceasingly to understand and to manage not life but those external material things. We are great geometers and artificers; we are great in our understanding of material things; but there is another greatness, a perceptual greatness, to which most of us have not attained, although it lies open to us, in fulness matching the fulness of our intellectual endowment.

We are not without plain indications of the existence in ourselves of that intuitive power, which as instinct is amazing to us in the accurate yet constrained lives of the beetles and the wasps. It is amazing chiefly because it is not that which we desire and are aware of desiring or needing to use. There is in every one of us, latent or declared, a true intuition of life, a truly intuitive awareness, a touch within, a perceptual knowledge sympathetic in the pure sense of the word, reaching far beyond the insect's. We may know it for what it is because in us giving rather than gaining is its secret spring, although gain, assuredly, comes by giving. Such, for example, is the knowledge of the artist, won only in his giving of himself to the object of his worship, in his placing himself by an artistic sympathy within it. Thus he obtains by sympathetic intuition an understanding that is like a spiritual touch, that is perceiving not thinking about, that, by immediate contact with the individual thing, is a knowledge of it in its own reality. Such again is the intuition of the true lover, who gives himself to the beloved and in that giving wins a knowledge like the artist's. They are akin, these two, artist and lover. Their kinship is grounded in their use of that intuitive character of life which for humanity as a whole has been cast into the shade by the more practically useful manners of intellect, and which in the insect-tribe is confined to the immediate needs of a fixed and narrow mode of existence.

Yet there is in truth a real difference, in these respects, between man and the insect or any other creature. In the perceptive consciousness of the insect, restricted by the fixed character of its nervous system, the intuitive potency of life has shrunk and hardened, as it were, into a restrained power which deals, and can deal, only with a very small part of life and the world. This power is forced to work in the windowless prison of a completed life. Man's life is not completed; in him consciousness, stretching out ever farther and farther, has passed one temporary limit after another, function impelling structure to match itself, mind seeking to go beyond itself. The consciousness of man has been always opening up for him new fields, adapting itself to new objects, moving among them, making a way through them, and in all its growth and change advancing in freedom. To attain this freed human consciousness seems, we may say, the motive principle of the evolution of life through man's forerunners. Its driving impulse is both carried indefinitely further in that consciousness and revealed as what it really is. Herein lies the difference in order between every animal, every plant, the most skilful of the beetles or the wasps, and man. Their way is closed. His lies before him wide open. He *is* the open way, the one open way on earth for life in its harmony of intuitive and intellectual power both fulfilled. And if hitherto we and our forefathers have in practice over-emphasized conceptual thinking and the intellect, our over-emphasis and its practical results have set us in a place where sympathetic intuition in perceptive experience has a new advantage. In us it will not, or rather it need not, be narrowed down. It may stretch out into every field that discursive and reflective thought has opened up, and it may pass beyond them to lead them on. The attainment by man of his high calling and of the destiny of which he is capable depends in truth on this expansion of his life. So the philosopher assures us. So, also—and this is noteworthy—does the psychologist: 'with the development of "psychical integration" both sides develop, and their relation, that is experience, therefore expands into a meaning inclusive of more and more, till, in the human being, it may be inclusive of all things actual and possible, the universe in space, and history in time from the remotest past, and, in imagination, to the most distant future.' The psychologist too, is not without his vision.

CHAPTER V

*If any one should care to say that unless I have
bones and muscles and the other parts of the body I
could not do what I would, that is well enough:
but to say that I act as I do because of them, and
that this is the way in which my mind acts, and not
from choice of the best, why, that is a very careless
and idle way of speaking.
Plato.*

There are signs that the life of the body is even in the lower
animals to some extent imbued with the free creative spirit.
There are creative efforts of determination, changes of
direction, triumphs over circumstance, that find their
enlightening context in the more emancipated life of man.

A sea-urchin's egg, for instance, begins its development by
dividing into two cells. Normally these cells, by a like
division, share between them the making of the respective
halves of the creature's body. If you remove one cell after the
first division of the egg you may expect (you certainly
should and will if you take your stand with the mechanistic
theorists) to find that you have mutilated the creature. You
may or will expect to see the remaining half of the egg grow
to a half-embryo. Under some circumstances you will see
what you expect; but if you are very skilful and are
acquainted with the new methods you will have the
disturbing joy of seeing the half-egg—you may even see a
quarter-egg—take on the work of the whole, and grow to a
complete though small embryo; and not only to an embryo
but to a larva. You may do the same with a newt's egg or a
frog's. With your mind's eye, then, you may if you like, and
if you thus interpret things, watch the sea-urchin's, the frog's,
or the newt's life, overcoming, according to a 'primary
purposiveness' of its own, your effort to thwart its intention.
You may watch it determining new contrivances from within

to meet an unexpected emergency that threatens to mar the complete whole it means to be, changing a normal to an abnormal course of activity, that it may still attain its end— in short 'working out its own salvation,' as a morphologist remarks, 'upon original and individual lines.'

It would seem difficult not to recognize in these changes a likeness to what you know in yourself as intelligent action. Studying them it is hard for any but a confirmed mechanist to resist the contention of men who tell us that the vital *is* the intelligent. Whereas purely material changes, if they are left to themselves, follow the way of least material resistance, life, whether in the cell or in the organism, moves in an opposite direction. The living vegetable cell raises carbon and other elements from relative inertness to a condition charged with newly available power. And in these developmental changes the organism seems to manifest itself as in very truth 'a living, active, responsive thing, quite capable of relinquishing at need the beaten track of normal development,' like ourselves as we make our bodily, intellectual, moral and spiritual decisions. The mechanist is ready with his retort when we say this, but it is a poor retort. He tells us of mysterious 'specific organ-forming substances' which are not ordinary chemical substances of any kind; and which no research is able to detect, except it be as pictured behind the very processes of growth that are telling *us* of the organ-forming determination of a specific mode of life. For both us and the mechanist there is the same process and result. He sees, but only with his mind's eye, these utterly mysterious 'substances' he has himself invoked; we see, with our mind's eye, the sea-urchin's, or the newt's, life issuing in that purposeful endeavour which always and everywhere, we say, is a mark of the life we know. We may even admit the possibility of the existence of his organ-forming substances, but only as conditions of life's organ-forming, not as effective causes—a distinction of fundamental importance for the careful thinker not content to be arrested by the look of things, however scientific. We cannot rest in a mechanical interpretation which at best only thrusts the problem one stage farther away, as does the pseudo-physicist-philosopher's ether-God. Life to us seems effective, and under all conditions determining, within the limits of those conditions. Organ-forming substances there may be; but they are either the co-operative servants of life (if they exist at all) like other substances, or they are no better than names for the modes in which life is at work. To us life seems, from its first entrance into possession of a body, when it gave to material substances a higher status, to have worked always towards dominance over the established laws and customs (that is the habits) of matter, as no substances have ever worked. At first it did little more with matter than lift physical or chemical elements upward in heightening states of energy, within a body, against physical or chemical tendencies that would take them downward to their physical or chemical equilibrium; later it went on, through the organizing of an ever more and more complex and variable nervous system, to a man's brain, where the control of intelligence over the living instrument that is its very active servant became strong enough to guide into ever-widening relations and possibilities an activity seeking spiritual advance. An activity, straining for liberation against some resistance by which nevertheless it was itself made effectual, could—we are driven to think—do no other than find its way imperfectly and by slow degrees; yet on its way it has shown even in very lowly creatures signs of what it really is. That any 'substance' the mechanist can acknowledge has done this of its own motion and power, we take leave to doubt. And we have learnt to understand the mechanist.

If the train of reflexion thus suggested is followed up, some of us will find ourselves compelled to readjust certain beliefs in regard to spiritual life as related to the life of the body, and in regard also to bodily life as related to the life of the spirit. We shall perhaps learn that in looking upon spirit as altogether separate from matter or as connected with matter only by some fortuitous or indeed unhappy link, we may indeed have kept it safe from the attacks of the materialist, but only at the cost of emptying it of value for ourselves, except in so far as it is, perhaps, an all but invisible *point de repère* round about which our vague religious sentiments are grouped. Just as in the evolution of elements and compounds afterwards united in the marvel of life-jelly, we traced the preparation of a pathway for life moving towards its first manifestation, so we should trace in the successive phases of that manifestation a development of co-operative relations between spirit and matter, a development rendering matter more and more plastic to spirit, and spirit more and more responsive to the character of the far from inert instrument through which its purpose is effected.

The evolutionist philosopher has told us that we may picture life as a rising wave opposed by the contrary movement of matter towards stability. The greater part of the whole volume of the wave, after reaching one height or another, is arrested; and going no further it is at each several height converted into the whirling eddies, the contented plants and animals of which we have already spoken. At one point only, where it rises highest, does the wave find a free passage (and of this too we have spoken) along which it carries with it, converted to its further purpose, the material obstacle, condition, and means that will, in a sense and for a time, still in some degree encumber, but cannot now arrest, its advance. The life-current continues to flow, a gathering wave of conscious life grown to self-consciousness and world-consciousness. It flows on from this point of conquest through generation after generation of men in and to whom its spiritual character is now plainly revealed. For each man it is a rill from the great human river of life—life natural and spiritual, spiritual because so fully natural—which has become his own and is indeed himself. For each the material but living brain is the chief instrument and helper by means of which he himself stretches forth towards wider and wider relations, not only with material objects but with other spiritual beings. And as the spirit of a man thus expands, amassing life and becoming, by the sympathetic spiritual inclusion of other lives, greater in its reach and in itself, it is confirmed and consolidated in its self-ownership. You may say that as a self-knowing, self-governing, creative being, an owner of means and a seeker after ends, man's life has at last taken possession of the kingdom of itself, and that it has reached this all-important status through the medium and condition of a body and by the experience of an earthly world.

We will let the philosopher tell us the gist of this in his own words:—

'While we watch the birth of consciousness we are confronted, at the same time, by the apparition of living bodies, capable, even in their simplest forms, of movements spontaneous and unforeseen. The progress of living matter consists in a differentiation of function which leads first to the production and then to the increasing complication of a nervous system capable of canalizing excitations and of organizing actions: the more the higher centres develop, the more numerous become the motor paths among which the same excitation allows the living being to choose in order that it may act. An ever greater latitude left to movement in space—this indeed is what is seen. What is not seen is the growing and accompanying tension of consciousness in time. Not only, by its memory of former experiences, does this consciousness retain the past better and better, so as to organize it with the present in a newer and richer decision; but, living with an intenser life, contracting, by its memory of the immediate experience, a growing number of external moments in its present duration, it becomes more capable of creating acts of which the inner indetermination, spread over as large a multiplicity of the moments of matter as you please, will pass the more easily through the meshes of necessity. Thus, whether we consider it in time or in space, freedom always seems to have its roots deep in necessity and to be intimately organized with it. Spirit borrows from matter the perceptions on which it feeds, and restores them to matter in the form of movements which it has stamped with its own freedom.'

Any philosopher, after writing or speaking some such words as these, may well ask us to consider—when we have watched the hard-won triumph of life over so great difficulties and so many obstacles, when we have discovered what seems to us clear evidence that it has for age upon age pursued with immeasurable power and resource a purpose which the spiritual consciousness of man is alone competent to fulfil, and that it has thus attained in man a position of supreme advantage for this fulfilment—whether we ought not to regard ourselves as paltering with reason if we expect that pursuit and that attainment both to be in vain. Is life, just where it seems in sight of final triumph, to be overcome at the last by death? Why should it be overcome by this when it has vanquished so much else? Why, if the world is rational, should we expect all the ages of preparation to be brought to naught, and the splendour of man's promise to be laid low in the grave?

We have to confess, I think, that reason is against this, and that when we allow ourselves to expect or to fear such an anti-climax we are influenced rather by prejudice, conscious or unconscious. Prejudice is born of our every-day dealing with things and our every-day notions about causes and about bodies. We think spirit is dependent upon matter, not as upon a living and responsive instrument of transmission and self-development to a certain necessary point of self-consolidation; but as most things we deal with depend upon other things, which, as we say, cause them, produce them, or make them do and be and happen. We suppose all too easily that just as steam ceases when the boiler-fires are drawn, so when the body dies life, its product, ceases too. We see the leaves fall from the trees to perish. *Tout passe, tout casse, tout lasse,*—it is the common lot of things and men. It is familiar—what more need be said? The burden of proof lies on the man who would tell us of exceptions to the rule.

Yet, if and when we come to examine things and men, do we discover any such rule applicable to men? Are we not all but compelled, reading the astounding story of evolution in the light cast upon it by its culmination in man, to question every uncriticized and easily formed opinion on a subject so complex and profound? If indeed there is evidence to show that life is neither produced by nor released from matter, but is in some sort conjoined with matter, lifting it from its own level, and using its powers in a way altogether different from their normal material course; if there is evidence that these powers are made to fulfil a purpose that can be no other than a purpose for life; then, obviously, matter, in the order of power and of nature, is life's subordinate. We must, indeed, as reasonable beings, correct those easy opinions—these things being thus. The similes and illustrations of every day do not fit the case. Intimate as is the relation between spirit and matter, there is no more reason to think life is produced by a material substance than to think the boiler-fire is produced by the steam. Both thoughts are equally absurd, and perhaps the chief cause of our thinking so easily the one and of our being quite unable to think the other is that we can see and touch boilers and the like, and cannot see and touch 'spirit and life.'

'Lamps burn in every house, O blind one! and you cannot see them.
One day your eyes shall suddenly be opened, and you shall see: and the fetters of death shall fall from you.'

CHAPTER VI
Within this earthen vessel are bowers and groves,
and within it is the Creator:
Within this vessel are the seven oceans and the
unnumbered seas.
Kabir.

When the brain dies it is resolved in the ordinary way
gradually, or may be resolved in a laboratory quickly, into
its constituents, which the chemist may collect as water,
carbonic acid and so forth, together with, roughly, a few
pinches of ash. Nothing is lost of what, as we say, it was
made of. After death it is left to fall from its temporary high
estate of power, and travel along the line of least physical
and chemical resistance to the low estate from which life had
raised its matter-stuff. Material necessity, such as we picture
it, then resumes its sway; physical laws, that is, let us say,
established physical habits, dominate once more.

But this brain, while human life employed and profited by it,
was in vital and structural continuity with the first life-jelly
that appeared upon the earth. You may trace, in the pictorial
scientific way, all its many cells to the germ-cell or egg from
which the whole body sprang. Again, and in the same
manner, you may trace this germ-cell, this egg, to another
from which it was derived. Some scientific men will tell you
that in every developing egg, during the very first stages of
its division, cells are set apart as germ-cells to continue the
race in the next generation. There runs, they will say,
through the generations of men a continuous underground
river-system of protoplasm, a continuous streaming of cells
from which are thrown up at intervals jets, as it were, of
living material which become individual lives. Or we may
put it that as in certain plants there is a creeping root-stock
hidden underground and giving origin here and there to new
specimens of the plant, so there is (according to this opinion)

a root-stock of germinative material passing on and giving rise to body after body, through all mankind. The source of this branching, interlacing germ-structure is in the beginnings of the world, and the beginnings of the world are—where? In the ether, the physicist may say. In the place and state from whence my elements have come, the chemist says. At present we, studying in these pages, are content to say that whatever the scientific details may be, the pathway of life that we see is one, from wherever the chemist and the physicist allow of a beginning to the place where both must own themselves confounded, the brain of man.

It is well to study that brain more carefully and try to relate it with the germ-cells of the protoplasmic streams from which it arose. We have to consider how it is that the brain of a son comes to resemble the brains of his parents, when the carrier of his parents' lives to him was only that fertilized germ-cell, a jelly with a nucleus, to all appearances no more. Here we must confine our study to one problem, that of memory, partly because we have no space for more, but chiefly because memory is an 'Open Sesame' to many wonders. We may if we please link it with heredity, with that passing on of characters and habits from parents to child through the comparative, but only comparative and very misleading, simplicity of the germ-cell.

'The man who could penetrate into a brain,' it is said, 'and watch what happens there would very likely see it full of sketched-out movements, there is no evidence that he would see anything else. He would have no more knowledge of what was going on in the corresponding consciousness than we should have of a play were we watching the comings and goings of the actors on the stage without hearing a word of it. If the play were no more than a pantomime the movements of the players would tell us nearly everything about it; if it were a comedy of life and manners they would give us next to nothing.' It has been said, too—and the simile is illuminating—that the brain is like a sort of central telephone exchange, permitting, delaying, or arresting communication. It is an instrument of analysis, of hesitation and of choice; but its office is said to be limited to the transmission and division of movement, movement started by things outside the body and movement started from within the body. The body is the conductor of these movements to and fro between objects acting upon it and objects upon which it acts.

Only in the form of motor contrivances do brain and body, we are told, store up the action of the past. This is a point of great importance in regard to both our own lives and our inheritance from our forerunners. We may distinguish two kinds of memory; one graven as it were in the living stuff of our body; another enshrined and active in the fluent personal history we ourselves most really are. Let us see what the evolutionist philosopher has to tell us about this. Let us illustrate our subject after his fashion.

In the matter of learning by heart, for example, there are two facts to be noted and two memories to be distinguished. When I know a poem by heart and can repeat it I say that I remember it. But I say also, perhaps, that I remember the stages by which I came to learn it. I remember, or may remember, occasion after occasion of my more or less successful repetition of the poem while I was learning it. I can recall, or may recall, step after step of my advance towards perfectly 'remembering' it. When it is learnt I say that it is imprinted on my memory; but I may also say that the steps of my progress towards knowing the poem are in like manner imprinted on my memory. Yet a very little thought shows that these are two kinds of memory, not one; and that there are two kinds of imprinting, not one. The memory of the poem itself has every mark of an acquired habit, even that of the disastrous effect of an interruption.

When I have repeated a poem for the twentieth time without mistake I may be thrown out of my declamatory stride by the banging of a door, and become unable either to tell myself how far I had gone in the poem or to pick up its broken thread. About a memory like this there is the mechanical look of an ingrained and almost unconscious habit. It is bodily, like the memory of a sonata for the pianist as he is playing, a memory which seems to him rather in his fingers than in his mind. But the memory of the steps and process by which I gradually learnt my poem is quite different. That is a history, not a habit. Each stage occurred only once; no one was graven into permanence by repetition, indeed no one was, or could be, ever repeated. Each was unique and had its own date in the history of the process and of my enduring life.

Here is a difference indeed to be reckoned with. There is a kind of memory that *represents* our past to us; and there is another kind (if it is memory at all) that *acts* it. I say, emphatically, if it is memory at all, this latter; for it does not really preserve the past, it only continues into the present an effect or a result of happenings of the past. In true memory history is preserved; the history of our whole lives is preserved in our true memory. But only the effects or results, only indeed certain effects and results, of the living real happenings in our living and real duration are graven in the body stuff as habits, as, if we like to call them so, habit-memories. The establishing of these memories is an affair of training and practice. The brain and body have to be forced into them; structure has to be shaped and taught, that it may carry on automatically, or all but automatically, some particular mode of action. And we note that the more nearly automatic these habit-memories are the better they work. When the nerve-paths in the structure of the brain and body are beaten smooth by treading and retreading the work goes easily and well.

There is nothing whatever of this kind about the true and unlearnt memory of events in our history, the memory which represents them. But just because the habit-memory is more immediately and constantly useful to us we notice it more. Indeed we frame on it our familiar conception of what memory really is, and come to regard the true memory of spontaneously arising recollections as only a bad example of the other. 'We ignore the fundamental difference,' so we are told, 'between that which has to be built up by repetition and that which is essentially incapable of being repeated.'

No doubt the two intermingle in every-day life and are therefore the more easily confused, not only by our every-day and usually careless selves but even by some careful thinkers. The confusion is dangerous for the thinker and the thinker in consequence becomes dangerous for us. Out of it has come in great part the unreasonable belief that a material brain is the storehouse of immaterial recollections, and that these after becoming either material or, in the physical sense, 'energetic' (as they must be to be stored in a material or 'energetic' way), in some altogether miraculous fashion at times take on consciousness and, as once more immaterial recollections, carry us into our own past. To say that motor-habits, with which when they are established consciousness may have little to do, can be registered in a flexible motor instrument and *acted* over and over again, is reasonable enough; but that conscious recollections can thus be registered is not only a gratuitous assumption unsupported by the facts of matter or energy or life, but is strictly incredible by any man who really knows and faces those facts. It is better to know and face them with the philosopher, and confess the reality of a spiritual life in which history endures, as well as the reality of a living instrument in which habits are established. No doubt an effort is required if we are to distinguish between the spontaneous and the habitual memories, between the memory of spirit and the habit-memory of its living instrument, the brain and body which together with the spirit are the man; but the effort is well worth making. It gives us a key to unlock many close-shut doors. When we try to learn something (as we are now about to do) concerning the problem of the transmission, through the succession of germ-cells, of the characters that mark out men—the problem of heredity—we find a conspicuous and very interesting use for it. But it has many uses besides that. We can use it with advantage in dealing with all the problems concerning the relations of spirit with matter.

Before we go on to deal with heredity we should note the value for our own lives of our ability to establish habits at all, to inscribe records of action in our instruments of body and brain which shall be capable of an almost automatic repetition. That is the way in which intellectual and bodily skill makes progress. We build a stairway too for our minds and spirits as well as for our bodies, when we lay down step after step of habitual action, handing over to it the carrying-on of what at first we had to think out, and then by degrees learnt to do skilfully and well almost without thought at all. That is the stairway by which the pianist advances towards a perfect execution of his music and the skater mounts towards perfect execution of a figure which at first was beyond his power. Throughout our lives we are handing actions over to be conducted by our bodies and brains as effects of work done consciously before, to be acted over and over again and pass beyond the need of conscious intervention, and in the end to be carried on the better without that aid. A man skates, or plays his violin, or writes a poem, or rides a horse, or walks, or dances, all the better when and if he does not have to think about the appropriate movements of his hands or feet or legs, or the necessary letters of his words, to all of which he once had to give minute attention. Perceptive and creative consciousness is thus set free. His mind, in its originality of creation and perceiving, is enabled to pour itself into the instrumental habit it has laid down and infuse it with his spirit, his poetic, musical, or athletic spirit. He may endow his motor instrument with his graces now that it works without his conscious aid.

We approach the problem of heredity from a new direction and with new eyes. Let us picture to ourselves (as has been suggested), instead of a succession of lives, a single life which goes on like the continuous germ-plasm of some biologists, and never grows old or dies. This one continuous life would pass through every stage of the succession of lives from the jelly-speck onwards. One immortal developing creature would accomplish (in our picture) the whole evolution from the original protoplasm to man. And this development would be effected by forming habits and rising step by step in and through and upon them. Is this in fact what actually has been done along the path of the ascent of species? That is the question which at once springs to our lips. Is heredity akin to the habit-memory which is preserved in our brains and bodies? There are men who tell us that the best conception of heredity they can form is something of this kind. They tell us that they think of individual lives as inscribing on germ-cells, by constant repetition, effects of what they have done. They tell us that the habit-memory of ancestral and thus communicated experience enables the baby to pump food into its mouth with that accurate adjustment of muscular means to exterior conditions and the principles of hydrostatics which it always shows. They go even farther and tell us that the development of any embryo from any egg is on the same lines of unfolding the habit-memories essential to its living as it does. Life in progressing from the single cell learnt, they think, by degrees, and consolidated its lessons into motor-habits graven in living stuff. Sometimes they point to the nucleus of the germ-cell as possibly the instrument for preserving these habits for other members of the race as the brain preserves less established habits for the man; sometimes they say that the cytoplasm acts in the same way. And whether we accept these suggestions or reject them we may recognize with some satisfaction that throughout the whole plan there runs the belief (or assumption—what you will) that function is primary, not structure, though structure once organized is the instrument and condition that contributes to the shaping of specific character.

Again we find ourselves both ready and called upon to emphasize the reality and the conservative office of matter, yet to regard it as subordinate to the reality and the initiative of life. We acknowledge once more the immeasurable import for life of its relations with matter. When structure is organized for function, when habit-memories become instrumental for life, function and life are in turn shaped by their instrument. Hence, probably, we have that condensed and fragmentary representation by the developing embryo of stages through which life passed slowly in epochs long ago, and during which (according to this hypothesis) it registered the fruits of its effort, by repetition after repetition, in the cell. The embryo chicken, the embryo child, both show in the course of their development signs (for instance the gill-clefts of the fish) of stages through which life had to pass before it became chicken or child life. But they pass very quickly from sign to sign. 'It took thousands of years to produce the first chicken, but the hen's egg reaches the same level in three weeks.' Each is obliged to pass these stages, it seems; the 'organ-forming substances' (as some say) of the germ-cell compel it, or (shall we carry our thought farther and say) the habit-memories recorded in it must be worked out lest the creature be brought to confusion; as the habit-memories of a pianist are and must be when he gives aright his rendering of the music he had learnt.

The memory-hypothesis concerning heredity does not involve the idea of compulsion or doom, it leaves room for the creature to work out its 'own salvation' on a basis inheritance supplies. It does not of itself regard the creature as doomed; whether the child or the chick is or is not doomed depends on what it is, that is to say, upon the character not upon the mode of its inheritance. Chick-character is one of doom; not so child-character. The child, starting from the point his race has reached as a race, may go on in virtue of an endowment of impulsive and creative power and a flexible brain and body absent in the chick. He may build his house of life, adorning or disfiguring his inheritance with a new-made character that is his own. This fruitful and interesting hypothesis of memory-inheritance may or may not stand tests that are to come. But we may accept it provisionally as what it is, sure that if it is displaced its successor will be more welcome still. That is the way of science; we pass always from good to better, from a guess that holds for one range of facts to another that holds for more.

CHAPTER VII

And is this life but the child of death? Then
blessed also be the word Death, the mother of life;
I will no more call thee Marah, but Naomi; for thou
art not bitter, but sweet; more pleasant, though
swifter in thy gait, than roe or hind.
Henry Montague.

In a world of creatures where the interests of each kind are
focused on the preservation of the species, and each
individual's attention and powers are in the main
concentrated on the pressing need for reproduction, and for
food and shelter to maintain life in itself and its young
progeny, conflict must ensue, a conflict of both ends and
means. Because, too, in these creatures the way of life is not
open, as in man, habit-memories may be taken as being the
chief agents for ensuring both species-life and individual
life, and as dominating both their history and their character.
Indeed the contracted world and the completed character of
such creatures with rare exceptions shuts out the interests of
other species. Hence the struggle for existence. Hence a
nature 'red in tooth and claw,' despite the general signs of a
love that of itself is ample prophecy of an enlargement
beyond the bounds of such restricted interests; despite also a
general and very obvious enjoyment of life for life's own
sake. We must not exaggerate either pain or its significance
in creatures who have neither our sensitive nervous system,
nor our ability not only to look forward and see
consequences and imagine our pain prolonged and growing,
but to increase that very pain by dwelling on it and exercising
in regard to it, more than it deserves, the magical power of
attention. Yet if we do not exaggerate, neither must we
ignore. Suffering, conflict, death are there and must be
reckoned with.

That the biologists of the latter part of the last century should magnify beyond due measure the place of natural selection in one regard, that of the origin of species, was to be expected. It was a great discovery; it filled men's minds. That they minimized, where they did not deny, the importance of the selective, determining and creative power of life itself was also to be expected. All this last was for the time obscured for want of evidence. Few men indeed, and those not biologists, then kept a level head. It is for this century to bring about a much needed balance in reckoning and in esteem.

Natural selection means for the most part a struggle ensuring the death of the weak and the 'unfit.' The survival of the fittest means that those creatures survive who are best adapted to all their circumstances, whether these are favourable or unfavourable to the maintenance of a high standard of living. That 'nature' may carry out selection it is necessary that there shall be no outside interference, say of man, able to stave off death, whether of the individual or of the race. Death, you see, is the protagonist in this biological play, or rather the mainspring of the machine. And, undoubtedly, death is not only conspicuous in nature but is of profound significance for life. Is it or is it not also of value in a sense surpassing that which the biologist acknowledges? Ought we to look upon it as the enemy or as the friend of life?

One thing is plain. Those men of science who saw it as protagonist were right in thinking that by the death, that is, by the natural selection, of the unfit from among the fit, the survival of useful variations may be assisted. Death, of course, cannot have anything to do directly with the originating of better lives (that is of better accommodated lives), but once they have come into being it can help to keep them in the ascendant as begetters of their kind. Natural selection has its use—shall we say its value?—for the advance of life.

Need we be surprised at this, we who have a more than scientific sense of values and have discovered purpose? Need we be surprised to find death a friend to life, seeing it everywhere? Matter is life's friend as well as means and hindrance. So too is death.

Let us consider the beginning of death on the earth; that is, of natural, not of merely accidental death. For it had a beginning, not coeval with the coming of life. There are living creatures now who normally escape it, who die only by accident, are, in fact, if they die, always killed. There are creatures alive now whose years are to be numbered by thousands upon thousands upon thousands, yet who have never grown old. The Pyramids of Egypt are of yesterday compared with the amoeba in the nearest pond.

The manner of life of a one-celled creature is this: it grows, and when it has grown to a size presumably inconvenient it divides into two creatures, both of which, obviously, are the same age. The creature itself becomes two instead of remaining one. The two creatures who were one repeat the process and become four. The four become eight and so on to the end of the earth. None die naturally, and when or if the end of the earth and of themselves is reached they will all be killed and every one of them will be of the same age; but none will be aged. They will be cut off, these naturally immortal creatures, in unimpaired maturity and the perfection of their structure and functions. But, you observe, if life on earth had not passed beyond the one-celled condition it would never, to our minds (if our minds could have been arrived at in some other sphere), have been worth living. All the potency and promise of life which have slowly been revealed through the improvement of its creaturely medium would have remained hidden behind the screen of those immortal jellies. Life began to create a new engine of advance when cell and cell were built up together, and the many-celled creatures started on their mortal and masterful career. For, note, the aggregation of cells in an organized body precludes their individual immortality. They become differentiated and associated for special purposes and they lose the opportunity of preserving life by continuous division. They are mutually imprisoning, they grow old, in time they die—they must die. Life, in beginning this advance, embraced inevitable death. Death, if you like, is the price—if indeed it should be counted a price and not a boon—that we pay for freedom to live as what we are and to become what we shall be. The immortal amoeba is after all a slave. It is this creature that manifestly pays a price, one at which no man of us would buy immunity from death.

There are many values and orders to be considered; and for the highest values and order of living, for the magnificent possibilities open to spiritual attainment, who would not barter an earthly immortality which should erect a barrier that spirit could not pass? But then we come to another consideration. Is death itself a barrier spirit cannot pass? All that I have written hitherto in these pages is directed towards an answer to that question. What should make us change the cumulative 'No' which our study of the processes and character of life forces to our lips? Already we human creatures, incomplete though we are, reveal life as an impulsive, enriching and creative power given in us and become ourselves—a power by which we may continue the line of a direct advance and pass on in a creative evolution which reasonably should have no end. What wonders may we not reveal, what wonders may we not discover thus, in that advance? But only if for the true life that is ourselves, the life which as ours is manifest in its use of body and brain and of the inheritance they bring, there is a triumph over the last of the many obstacles it encounters upon earth. For, let there be no mistake, the immortality of the race upon earth, even if it be possible, is not enough to satisfy reason and accord with the promise of every individual man as what he is for himself, and in his own special relation and contribution to the well-being of the whole. Each man becoming as he should become has his own peculiar value, each his own spontaneity and continuous creative power. If he is lost all this comes to an end, and the world of men is the poorer for want of what he might have given. There is no shifting of our reasonable demand for the conquest of death from the individual man to his race, even if (as is not so much as probable) his race does not die in the cooling or drying or heating of his earth.

After all, what is 'this body of death' from which every man must part? It is, we declare, his medium of transmission and the motor and sensory instrument and condition by means of which he had both inherited a foundation upon which to build his own life, and entered into relations with an outside world of things and persons. Chemically and physically it is a stream of particles always passing away, always being renewed, at one rate or another. The few particles unchanged during his life are not actively sharing his life; they are only its physical supports. Whatever shares his life changes. This stream that his food and the air and the water make, he takes up, transforms, uses and dismisses. All his life long he is dying bodily, and is growing, or should be growing, spiritually. Death is for him the finishing of a process in his body that has always gone on, the final casting away of material elements he has always cast away when he had done with them. And meanwhile, in the spiritual duration of his life, its minister the body has consolidated his self-conscious unity, so that he dies, or should die, a true owner of his real and true and valuable self. For this end earthly life seems to the eye of reason ever to have been striving. Is its striving to be finally in vain? Everything that we have considered in these pages declares the unlikeliness of that.

Is a man then to pass from this world bodiless, as some of the ancients thought? To be able to offer a tentative answer to this question we must go back to one of our earlier chapters and remind ourselves of the ether which, the physicist says, interpenetrates all the molecules of our body now, and is the medium of communication everywhere through the systems of the worlds. May I think of the ether, then, as being in my body the medium of communication between me, as spiritual life and consciousness, and the material elements and structures of my body? If the comparatively coarse granular matter of the chemist's colloids and the protoplasmic speck shows such a congruity with my life as makes it fit to live in me and be the bearer to me of ancestral habits, may I not think that a still closer congruity exists between this ether and my life? And, again, is it not possible, or even likely, that it is through the ether of my body that I influence its matter and its matter influences me? If these things are so, then my ether-body is more fully mine and more closely bound to me than is my matter-body. I think of myself passing at death into, or discovering myself in, an ethereal country where my ethereal body shall serve me even better than my matter-body serves me in this matter-country. And if this thought seems the plain man's plain thought about the physicist's hypothesis and is condemned for that, I retort that the plain man through his rejection of constraint by specialism, and by ideal or abstract schemes which flout the wholeness of experience, is coming now into his own in science, in philosophy and in religion. He has his rights and is taking possession of them in a new fashion and with new significance.

One thing more I think of. The physicist says that what he calls 'bound ether,' that is ether within the spaces of a material thing, differs in its character from the free ether of the interstellar spaces. He has been able to prove this, he says, by experiments on the transmission of light through ether 'bound' in water.

What more do I want? The ether changes in character from association with matter in a body. I see it in my mind's eye changed by constant association with my brain and limbs and with my active consciousness as it could never be changed in water. Am I right, I wonder? Shall I see some day how it has been changed? Shall I see my more intimate body revealed and know it and myself raised to high estate?

However this may be, the life that made for itself body after body on earth, conquering the habits and reluctances of matter that it might use it for a spiritual purpose, is possessed of a creative and organizing power to which no man should dare to set bounds, and which by me at least shall be trusted to the end. That which builds from the egg the chicken, and from the first jelly-specks all the races of the globe, must still be capable of looking after me—if I am worth it.... I am bold enough and plain man enough to say with the poet,—

'Into the audience hall by the fathomless abyss
where swells up the music of toneless strings I shall
take this harp of my life.'

CHAPTER VIII
The soul needs only to open the door.
Boehme.

By the establishing of habit-memories in the nervous structures of man consciousness is liberated for another and, if the man will, a nobler use. The instrument may be forgotten, the work goes on. This liberation of the spirit from attention to modes of activity and actions that can be automatically or almost automatically carried on is among life's greatest triumphs. And the triumph is indefinitely extended in man's peculiar relation to his tools, and through the peculiar character of both his tools and his tool-making.

An animal's tools are parts of its body; they are stings, claws, fangs and so on. Some of the tools of man are also parts of his body; but there are others, not his natural organs, by which its instrumentality is extended—and that, you may say, without signs of coming to an end. It seems as though life had a sort of prophetic instinct in this business; for primitive man was driven to search for these new tools by his lack of organic armament of either the offensive or the defensive kind. He had no protective shield like the armadillo or the crab; and even the scanty covering of hair, which contrasted so ill with the close fur of his cousins, grew scantier still, until it became altogether useless against rain or cold or storm. He had no claws, no tusks, worth considering as weapons of offence; but he had a desirous and adventurous mind, and both by his necessities and his mind he was driven to the making of tools. He owned also one very remarkable natural tool. He had an archaic five-fingered hand inherited from his amphibian ancestors, which had not been specialized into a wing or a shaft ending in a hoof or a paw—a hand plastic, mobile, delicate and sensitive, a very 'instrument of instruments' for a creature opening wide the gate for life.

We are apt to think of this beautiful tool of ours as highly specialized. It is not; it was preserved unspecialized from the amphibian stage throughout a long pre-human history, as though life had indeed foreseen just what was coming and knew that its versatility would make it the worthy partner of man's versatile brain. Let us put it that way. (Or let us say that it was a happy accident. As you please; anyhow the fact remains.) The result was that man possessed a natural tool beautifully adaptable for making and using many and various artificial tools. And there was not another creature upon earth that had not either spoilt its hand for those various uses by specializing it for some narrow use, or like the monkeys and the apes, had no brain to match. Man specialized his feet, as the monkeys and the apes did not; he left his multifarious hand alone.

By means of this hand he projected into space the powers of his body and his mind. He began, no doubt, with sticks and stones; he went on to strings; and from sticks and stones and strings he passed to telescopes with which he reached new stars, spectroscopes with which he saw what they were made of, telegraphs and telephones through which his speech and hearing stretched out from land to land, and destructive machines by which his delicate fingers shattered and blasted with the power of a thousand storms. These things and more he has done; and all the tools he has used are extensions of both his body and his mind. So too are the industrial machines by which he manufactures (note the word) what his newly-complicated needs demand of clothes and food and furniture and the like. So too are the astounding machines which make for him other and different machines. And everywhere we see that in the advance of his tool-devising he draws nearer to making those which will work either without his aid or with very little of it. His tools grow more and more automatic, more and more saving of the labour of mind. He makes, you may say, artificial habit-bearers, motor-structures by which the devices of his mind are carried into action independent of his mind, as other devices are through his nervous system and his muscular limbs. Thus he follows the example set him by life in its organizing of living tools. And we ought to tell ourselves (parenthetically) at this point that the one reasonable and worthy use of all our machinery is just this—to follow the example of life not only in the actual organizing but in the purpose and meaning of organization. We ought to acknowledge to ourselves that unless our machinery liberates the mind and spirit of man to serve better and more freely his spiritual needs it will of a certainty enslave him. At present, because most of us are in the dark as to the direction in which life strives to conduct us, machinery is used to emancipate the few and to enslave the many. We do not know what we are doing, we do not understand what the primacy of spirit means or should mean for us all. We do not know how we ought to grow, every one of us, in the natural, that is, in the spiritual way.

Why do I venture to say that in the spiritual way we *ought* to grow? And what in fact is that spiritual way? Do life and experience point out the way and emphasize the 'ought'? Here we come to the gist of our whole inquiry.

If in looking back along the road on which, in these chapters, we have been trying to pick out stage after stage, we discern a governing purpose and the foreshadowing of an end; and if we also discern not only the possibility but also the means, through intellect and intuition, through action and feeling and thought, of identifying ourselves with that purpose and throwing the energy of our own lives into furthering it, we shall see both the ought and the way. We shall dimly discern, too, the promise of the end, although we do not and cannot yet know what we shall be. From the moment when the life-current driving onward and overcoming one by one the reluctances of matter along the genealogical ascent to man, reached him—*homo faber*, the skilful tool-maker, *homo sapiens*, the able thinker—from that moment the sublime purpose of all that had gone before began to be revealed.

The advance of life's main stream in all its variety of operation shows, from the beginning until now, one character and motive-principle. It begins, as we have said, by subduing to its purpose the inveterate habits of material elements, those habits we speak of as physical necessity and law, raising their status that they may be servants in new power to a freedom foreign to themselves. From subduing and assembling elements within cells it passes to the assembling of cells and lifts up these in their turn to higher place. They play their part in a commonwealth; they are servants whose habits, like those of matter, further the cause of a freedom they cannot reach. Their own relative necessity is subdued and used through their coöperating. They promote what they neither see nor know. Finally they reach their highest function in a man's brain, where they coöperate to carry power to an incalculably various use. There it is that life, by a very splendour of new emancipation, passes, as the philosopher says, 'through the meshes of necessity,' passes through that net the cords of which it has itself both spun and knotted from the refractory substance of material things.

Man comes into his heritage. He inherits, we may allow ourselves to say, from the habits of elements and from the habit-memories of cells, single and corporate. He inherits from the habit-memories of every living creature in his ancestry. And each habit-memory of them all has contributed to his setting free. Now he is so far master that life has put into his hands the choice between a greater freedom still towards which its impulsive purpose has been directed from the first, and a new slavery that the man himself is able to make for himself. For—and surely we need to note this for our warning—the conduct and determination of life, which is in some small measure in the power of every creature within its manner of life, is given over to man; and the next step in emancipation is for him to take or leave as he will. He may dominate the whole chain of habits and go forward; or he may wind it about him and entangle his spirit in its fetters.

Matter, his body, the habits or habit-memories he inherits or makes for himself, all these may either be instruments of his growing liberation or machines that turn him to the likeness of themselves. The pianist who has wrought his music into the living instrumentality of his fingers may leave his fingers to work as mechanism, or he may pour into their established habit the riches and beauty of an artistic soul. Thus it is with all the heritage and possessions of a man. He may submit to them as to a constraining mechanism and grow mechanical himself, or he may infuse them with his spirit and raise them and himself to that further altitude which spirit seeks. We may well say of some men that they are the slaves of habit; we may well think more than we do of the many kinds of habit to which men may be slaves.

To look on heredity as an affair of transmitted habit-memories is to discover our true relation with it, once we have come to see what the spiritual memory of an enduring and accumulating spiritual life, lived according to its proper meaning, may be for man. In the chick the inherited habit-memory of its race is as the boundary wall of cellulose is for the plant-cell; in the child it is a standing ground from which, while his creative spirit stirs within him, he surveys the kingdoms of a world. In the man, like the habits he himself builds up, it may come to be a hill-top from which he looks down upon all those kingdoms and their glory. Life incurred death when first the cells were summoned out of solitude to work together in a body. And here, too, it is as though it foresaw what was coming, saw in a vision a creature come to being who should have life in himself and be divinely discontent, seeking to go on. It is hard to think that a creative impulse beginning so low down, so humbly, and yet purposive enough and skilful and potent enough to reach the immeasurable wonder and promises of man, should ever have been blind, or in the last resort should be no more and no greater than himself.

CHAPTER IX

The human animal desires to escape from its
animal prison by means of all kinds of love, by
freedom of emotion no less than of action and thought.
And it attains to the freedom of emotion when it is
aware of beauty. It cannot be aware of beauty
except in self-forgetfulness, and it cannot produce
beauty except in self-forgetfulness.
Arthur Clutton-Brock.

No doubt the great question for any man in regard to
himself—if he is able and willing to put one so searching—
is whether he is or is not on the way to aid in the fulfilment
of the promise of life. It is a question hard to answer, for the
promise of life grows ever greater in our eyes once we have
begun to see it at all. There was a time when for our ancestors
of the caves it must have called for little more than strength
and skill, courage and perseverance, in attack or in defence
and in the procuring of shelter, food and wives. The bitter
struggle in which they were engaged was a real struggle for
existence in which every man must fight for his own hand,
or at best for his little group of near kindred. There were not
many differences then between the practical demands of the
daily life of men and those of the daily life of the hyenas or
the wolves. But there were other differences, and they were
great and significant. One in particular has left a wealth of
evidence behind it, evidence graven and painted in certain
caverns. There are bisons, for example, painted by some of
the men whom we call primitive, or savage, which are of the
truest art. There is no such difference and no such likeness
between those bisons and the artistic work of to-day as there
is between the flint-headed arrow and the machine-gun. The
arrow and the gun are products of an intellectual ingenuity,
practising and becoming expert through practice and
concentrated on the external relations of thing with thing; the
painting comes of a direct intuition of the reality and the

essential beauty in a bison's life. They are alive for us, those bisons, and they are beautiful. Their creator was a true artist, able to throw himself into the object he wished to discover, to feel and to depict; and he was able to endow his picture with the bison's life and his own. If you are in aesthetic sympathy with him you can feel the creature he paints as you feel the man painting. The intellect that devised the arrow has always to travel onward by an accumulating process, from step to step; the intuition that felt the bison arrived at once. No doubt there is not only intellect but intuition in the arrow; and there is not only intuition but intellect in the painting; but the emphasis and the proportion are contrasted in the two.

Why did this primitive artist paint at all? There are those who suggest that he had some practical end in view to be reached by the magic of representation—an idea perhaps of thus ensuring luck for his hunting. But at least that can hardly be true of the graceful form and the conventional adornment he gave to some of his tools. It is far more likely that even if he began with magic and a practical end he went on to paint for the pure joy of it, the pure spiritual joy of inspired admiration glowing to a creative act, and winning admiration in its display. That is the manner of art—even to the delight in its being admired by those to whom it is made known—and this man's work is the work of an artist. I should say these men's work is the work of artists, for there were many of them in many generations. There was not merely a single eccentric genius—though even one would have sufficed us for a revelation. Here then, in these caverns, we have a kind of work done by many men, who, however much they looked for admiration from their fellows, worked in something of the self-forgetfulness of an artist; so we may presume. The man who pursued it did not in any lesser way profit by it (unless his fellows were self-forgetful enough to pay him for the joy he gave, and that only extends and strengthens the case); but he assuredly profited in his spirit, which there found its outlet as creative, there showed its self-forgetting love of something beyond self, there in consequence found its joy. The true artist paints or sings for the love of it, and because he must; and wins his joy, even though in and with the artist's pain, and the man's self-seeking. The spirit within him drives him on; no outward necessity, no carnal attraction, no mere self-seeking, is adequate to force or draw him. Art, however skilled and taught, however marred by human weakness, is spontaneous as love. We are in presence here of that of which only faint adumbrations can be discerned in any other creature than man. There are adumbrations; and there is at least a plain foreshadowing of love. But full and lasting self-forgetfulness is to be attained only in man, and true art and true love, like true joy, depend upon it.

The declared promise for the further advance of life in us demands and displays growth in self-forgetfulness. The man who strikes us as being above other men is one who shows us powers other men either have not or do not use, and uses them as other men very often do not use them. He is always stamped with the stamp of spirit. He is creative and he is self-forgetful. We do not really, or at least readily and spontaneously, admire any man who does things from self-interested motives. We may admire the things he does, but we do not admire the man. If, for example, we are religious ourselves, and however much we wish other people to be so too, we do not admire the man who, we know, is religious because he sees his profit in religion either for this world or the next. We do not admire the kind of artist who clutches at beauty because it feeds that deadly appetite which is no other than aesthetic greed. We want him to admire a beautiful thing for its own sake, because it is what it is and is altogether admirable. And no lover holds our respect if for him his beloved is merely a curio to be proud of or a satisfaction of the flesh. We say justly that he is only a lover of himself. To command our admiration a man must stretch out his desire and enlarge his interests beyond the boundary of self; he must give himself, not necessarily without reward—for the joy set before him often comes—but without making the attainment of it a motive spring.

That simple fact proves the spirits that we are. And it is shown in strange places. Even the leader of the gang of thieves wins admiration by his carelessness of personal gain. Robin Hood is always both honourable and honoured, though he steals.

Think then how much life had gained in power of expression when the painters of the caves were reached. Yet the philosopher reminds us that indeed this gain began with the beginning of love. Self-forgetfulness began before man came to show himself called by spirit and life to die daily. Yet in and by him they call with an emphasis and solemnity new in the tale of creation. He is to die to the struggle and the desire to live; he is to give himself and grow by self-giving. That is his proper way.

Not without reason does the philosopher tell us that the supreme secret of life begins to be revealed in the plant which surrenders its own life for its seed. But if we ignore the far plainer voice of man, how can we hear what has been whispered by the plant? If we are made mechanical by slavery to our own tools how can we discern either? And unless we listen with the ears of our intuitive soul we shall never hear what it is that they are saying. Unless we immerse ourselves in the current of the spirit, unless we confide ourselves to the life that would bear us on, we shall miss the fulfilment of our promise. The whole long weary road of life has been travelled on our behalf in vain, unless through the adventure of self-giving we become unceasing spiritual creators of greater selves than those we are now.

CHAPTER X
If thou hast union now, thou shalt have it hereafter.
Kabir.

Without social life no one of the peculiarly human powers of a man comes to fruition. He may chatter, for example; he cannot speak. He has all the necessary organs and all the necessary power, but man-language is part of an inheritance stored up for him in community life. It is stored up there, just as clinging with his hands and sucking with his lips are stored up ready for him at birth, in his body. Society is for him an immense extension of his body, and therefore a further means of extension for his spirit. It is also an immense extension of the bodies and spirits of other men with whom he may enter upon relations. You may look on it as supplying a brain common to all men which all may use together, and in which their activities should find not only a recording medium but an unfailing stimulus and contributory aid. But the social brain is in a peculiar sense men's own making, as free and capable creators. They have come to be owners of life and directors of its course in a degree they certainly had not attained when their bodily brains were slowly growing to be what they are. This brain of theirs, used in community, is as truly built by their own efforts as are the houses in which they live. The evolution of man has to all intents of spirit ceased to advance by changes in his body, but it goes on by incessant change and enormous amplification in his community life.

Here, too, in this many-bodied and many-souled community, as well as in the individual man's life, function determines structure. But function has there become self-conscious and world-conscious, aware of the many bodies and the many souls, aware of their needs and dangers, aware of their giving and their gaining. Men have societies within the community such as on the whole their conscious desires and purposes, their attitude towards their fellows, their sense of responsibility and obligations, their aims and ideals, demand. We have indeed the societies we deserve. We may well ask ourselves why we deserve to have them as they are; we may well say to ourselves—'"Prisoner, tell me, who was it that wrought this unbreakable chain?"' And the answer is clear, convicting not only of error but of what some of us have learnt to know as actual sin, sin against the call and promise of life. '"It was I," said the prisoner ... "when at last the work was done and the links were complete and unbreakable, I found that it held me in its grip."'

There are other societies besides those of men. Some are far more completely organized. The bees and the ants have carried social organization to a state of harmony and of adjustment to ends which is as strongly marked in its contrast with any that human societies present, as is the triumphant surgery of the solitary wasp by contrast with the blunders of an untrained man. In 'the civility of these little citizens' society is carried to a completeness corresponding with that of the life of the creatures who are its parts. In an ant-hill or a hive we have before us, some may say, a model of what a society should be. Perfect co-operation, complete subordination of individual to social ends, the highest possible working efficiency of each and all—it sounds well, and no one can deny that for bees and ants it works well. Would it work equally well for men?

The answer we give to this question will depend on two things. It will depend first on whether we think that men are or are not competent to advance, and are aided to advance, as beings not only spiritual in essential character and purpose, but self-creative and so able to reach both an efficiency beyond all constraint by institutions and machines, and an enlargement of community-life which shall embrace society upon society in all their diverse modes. Secondly, it will depend on whether we are or are not willing to organize any society by what used to be called biological methods, that is by the methods of the arena—of the 'gladiators' show.' If we decide on the gladiators' show and a social efficiency with no further outlook than a highly superior human ant-hill's, we pronounce ourselves believers that in principle the ant-hill manner of life with its isolation of society from society will work for men. We may be wrong even in a short view or a narrow view of man's capacities and existence; we are certainly wrong if spiritual progress lies before him as a glorious prospect not only for this man or society of men here, or another there, but for all men as members of an all-containing community made one only by an all-containing principle. In face of the promise and adventure of life we are as certainly wrong in giving consent to the ant-hill principle for society as we should be if we consented to exchange our own pregnant incompleteness for the perfection of the ant. Yet we of the modern civilized nations of Europe and America have been far too much influenced of late years, not only by our animal inheritance and the passions that we share with 'ape and tiger,' but by what is now a powerful tradition and in the last century was a new force—the mechanistic conception of social life. Our reasoning about society, our social science, even our social practices, have by this tradition been made not only more materialistic—many of us know that—but more plausibly mechanistic. It has seemed to us that we have science and nature both on our side, in trusting less to the initiative of life and more to its organization of circumscribed institutions and ordered means. We have taken a biological hypothesis far too seriously. And no doubt we have done this in great part because it has enabled us to leave uncriticized, or even to justify, habitual ways of acting and thinking which have about them still the taint of the pit from which we have been digged. These ways of ours were laid down for us in the long effort of each man to keep his footing on earth for himself and for the few he recognized as his own; but we have made them both more difficult and more dangerous by loading ourselves with a burden of perverted or artificial needs which not only call for perverted or artificial means to satisfy them, but set us in opposition to other men from whom we wrest their satisfaction. Those ways and this burden are proper to a creature who in very truth is seeking so to encumber life as to prevent its carrying him on, so to contract his own life as to prevent its intermingling with the lives of others. In short they are proper to one who is arresting life in himself as it has been arrested in the tiger or the ant. It will be arrested at a higher point—that is all; and it will be consciously arrested by the conscious building up of an obstacle far more serious than death. Therefore it is no mere failure; it is sin—sin against the true nature of human life.

The mechanistic theories of biology, which have helped to confirm men in an evil course, are fast being discredited. With them will go a false philosophy which has been widely current of late and has had an influence reaching far beyond an acquaintance with its authors' names. Critical and careful biologists are now undoubtedly doing much to effect this salutary change. Yet, may be, we shall be driven to call some of their opponents (as has been prophesied) by the bad name of necrologists, that we may perhaps shock them into self-knowledge. It is a name only too grievously appropriate now, since the picture of natural evolution they have, all innocently, drawn has not only foreshadowed, but contributed to fill, the grave-yard of the peoples dug in the great war.

We are changing this baleful picture; we are learning too, partly in consequence, that the self-interest of utilitarian economists and the ruthless search for individual advantage which social mechanists have commended are not the mainsprings of evolution. Of far greater, more lasting, and more profound significance and effect than the self-interested struggle for existence among animals and plants has been the species-interest to which self-interest has been subordinated. A creature must first eat and only afterwards reproduce; but this in no way justifies us in thinking that competition for food is charged with more meaning in the long story of life than the protective care of parents for their offspring and the eminently natural self-sacrifice it involves. Progress among both animals and vegetables has been secured more by 'species maintaining' efforts than by a mere self-seeking struggle for self-restricted ends. It is a recognition of this fact that makes a distinguished biologist say, 'The ideal of evolution is thus no gladiator's show, but an Eden; and although competition can never be wholly eliminated ... it is much for our pure natural history to see no longer struggle, but love as "creation's final law."'

PART II

CHAPTER I

If the doors of perception were cleansed, everything
would appear to man as it is, infinite. For man has
closed himself up, till he sees all things through
narrow chinks of his cavern.
Blake.

As we looked at chlorophyll, at colloids and the sea-urchin's
egg, so let us look at Christian habits and beliefs. And in the
first place we will fix our attention on the central 'mystery'
of worship in the Christian Church. All the world over and
from the first days of Christian apostles and brethren, a man
going into one of their places of assembly would at some
hour or another find their devotion apparently gathered about
common, familiar, bread and wine, or, sometimes, bread
alone. They would tell him that this bread 'is no longer
common bread.' Nevertheless, in the ordinary or the
scientific sense, it is, just as much 'common bread' as
chlorophyll is the common colouring matter of the green
wheat. They will tell him, too, that it is a 'sacramental' means
of communion between God and themselves and between
them and Christ, the Anointed Son of God. Just as we insist
scientifically upon the fact that chlorophyll is the meeting-
point between the power of the sun and our living selves, so
Christians insist that the sacramental bread, whatever else it
is or does, constitutes a meeting-point between them and
God and his Christ. No doubt (they may say, if they
understand such matters), for the mathematical physicist,
bread, like everything else, may be finally reduced to a series
of dynamical equations. Or it may be taken as ether and
electrons; or as hydrogen, carbon, oxygen and so forth; or,
roughly, as what it comes to be at last, gases, water, and dust,
like the bodies of us all. But each of these ways of looking
at bread manifestly, even to the mind of that scientific man,
leaves out something of its richness and fails to reckon with

its use and purpose for life. By ordinary persons it is known as the 'staff' of life; and these ordinary persons, when they say it is this, are speaking poetry. In fact if you are to do justice to bread you must be something of an artist; you do it gross injustice—that is, you leave out of your account the most valuable thing about it—when you do not go beyond the scientific man's idealistic or abstract summing up. The poet's vision does better when he mates in the corn and the grape the glories of the sun and the expectancy of earth, and sees the bringing forth and revealing and communicating, through the grain and the wine, of a concealed and straining life. But the philosopher also has his contribution to a fulness of justice. He insists, after his manner, on 'spirit and life'; he disdains mechanism; he opens gates that science cannot pass, and shows that all real things have depth it cannot reach—a third dimension where it has discovered only two. He solidifies the schematic diagrams of the scientific man and gives reasons for the faith of the religious man, who goes further still.

Here in the Christian Sacrament, where the Christian says that the fullest justice is done to bread and wine in lifting them up to be a means of communion between God and man, science and philosophy, religion and art, may meet together.

For nearly two thousand years Christians have seen in 'this bread' of theirs matter impenetrated by spirit, and raised by it into another and a higher order. They have held to a doctrine of both in which neither was despised, or thought of as deceiving or unreal. Materialistic thought and theory, abstract spiritualism, all theories or doctrines that cut the world of experience in two with a rationalizing hatchet, have been powerless to loosen their hold. Matter informed and transformed by spirit; spirit pre-eminent over and including matter—these have been cardinal and inevitable implications in the sacramental worship of Christians.

Cardinal and inevitable, too, is, in consequence, their view of the world as an affair of order superposed on order in a nature capable of being raised to the height of that which they call the supernatural, an earth that may become a new earth, a city of men that should rise to the noble state of a City of God.

We look back on the chemist's colloid that becomes, as protoplasm, no longer common colloid but one from which a world of living creatures has arisen. We see again a wonderful life informing and transforming matter, pre-eminent over it yet dependent on and manifesting through it. We see the chlorophyll of the plant raising chemical elements to a new order of being, and life in its onward march from order to order of manifesting consciousness, attaining at last man, creative in his spiritual freedom and dominance. We see that a Christian might point to man himself as the summing up of outward and visible signs and an inward and spiritual grace which science has made known, as reasonably as he may take bread as the central symbol of his worship. And he may tell us, or we may tell him, that these things are one—that there is everywhere 'continuity of process with the emergence of real differences' in a world that is 'sacramental' from its lowest to its highest order, from the speck of jelly to man. He and we both may see it as a world of outward and visible signs, each manifesting what the Christian names 'an inward and spiritual grace,' and we name—how do we name it? So far, only *life*, mysterious and mysteriously potent, communicating and communicated life.

We are encouraged to consider, further, this name and its meaning for us and above all in us. In us, we justly say, life is really different from what it is in the plant. We are 'persons'; plants are not. Life in us is personal, in the plant it is less than personal. But it is life, all the same and all through, from the impersonal to us, different though we assuredly are from the impersonal. And we can hardly escape asking ourselves whether, as they are now, men are of the highest order of real difference among the different orders embraced in the potency of life. Can life do no more and better, seeing that it has done so much? Is it, in itself, no more and better? The Christian answers these questions without one moment of hesitation. He says that 'the Holy Ghost,' the divine Spirit and Lord, is the 'Giver of Life'; and that there is an order of life in which this Lord and Giver is brought into personal relations with us, communicating with and communicated to us; so that by this communication we are raised beyond the state of children of earth and of the merely earthly life, to the high place of Sons of God, who know their Father and are at one with each other and with him.

If there is a thorough-going evolutionist anywhere it is the Christian. And it is his sacramental doctrine that gives consistency and persistence to his evolutionary convictions, if and when they are consistent and persistent. At times they are neither. At times the Christian, like the rest of us, fails to see the grandeur and universality of his own deepest principles. And then he belies them in word and deed; and his picture of the world of men and things is false to them and to himself.

It is these deepest principles that the enquirer should search out. When he has caught one glimpse of them he should thereby be strengthened against the falsifications that are offered him either by Christians or their contemners. Great principles are there, for his vision and enlightening. And in them he will find his own raised to a higher power. His evolution is then carried beyond the point where it so abruptly and unsatisfactorily breaks off. His potent life is there borne upward to the meeting-place with a Lord and a Giver of life. His personal, self-conscious and world-conscious, loving and self-sacrificing man, the crown of his evolutionary process, comes face to face with the source and fulfilment of all that he is and all that he so brokenly promises to be. Man himself crowns the sacramental world and is its greatest sacrament, revealing as in a glass darkly and by foretelling, the fulness of beauty and glory in all its grace. And the Christian points to one man as above all other men in the revealing office of mankind. He says that this man in no way distorts the beauty and glory given him; that in him very God is made known in and as very man. Here, plainly, the sacramental principle reaches its supreme height, and is taken beyond detail after detail to a wholeness covering every detail. If any one man is thus the unclouded revelation of God in terms of man, then it is true—as the Christian says it is—that the whole world of men and things is best, most faithfully and fully, stated, reasoned about, interpreted, through this man. Every particle of the bread we eat becomes for us no longer 'common bread.' It is bread shown for what it really is in the plan and process of God as these are made present to us, alive, pregnant of glory and beauty and power, in the living revelation of Jesus Christ.

The Christian sets his consecrated bread apart from all the rest of bread and things, and, we must own, he does well. For men see all things as in a glass darkly, and we are, most of us, the slaves of habit and victims of familiarity. What is everywhere and always soon comes to be nowhere and never for our interest and our attention. If the Christian had not kept as a rare thing, a thing enthroned, the bread that is for him no longer common bread, he would of a certainty often, if not for ever, have lost hold on the sublime principle it enshrines for him and for the world. The conflicting currents of speculative thought, as well as the weaknesses of his mental grasp, would have made him loose his hold upon it. Just because it stands there as the central symbol gathering up and establishing his worship and its sanctifying associations, it has lasted through the centuries, preserving its own great principle, a witness, a token and a sign not empty but 'effective'—*signum efficax* not only for thought but for all human life in its amplitude.

CHAPTER II

Can you think at all and not pronounce heartily
that to labour in knowledge is to build up Jerusalem,
and to despise knowledge is to despise Jerusalem
and her builders?
Blake.

For the Christian a man is a being capable of receiving and assimilating life as no other creature can, and as the biologist has no biological reason to believe. The Christian declares that he has reason, good and ample. He *knows* whom he believes. This is a matter of living religious experience to which generations after generations have borne witness. There is a ladder of spiritual reality, he says, up which men are climbing and upon which some have reached great heights. The biologist's ladder, despite its many steps and its length along the ages, is too short for him. Or rather (so he will tell you when he understands what the biologist means) his own ladder is a legitimate and even a natural extension of that, as of all others of the sort that men have anywhere set up.

Is this advance of man, then, an affair of a single departmental business—the religious business? Or, let us ask, can there be kinds of knowledge that are not really knowledge of God? Is it reasonable to regard biological knowledge, or chemical or physical, as knowledge of some alien reality not embraced in God? The supposition is monstrous. If God is, then all truth attained by man is truth of him. If I learn that the world advances from the ether to my brain I shall have learnt something about God. So the Christian should maintain, if he is true to his Christian principles. The advance of man towards communion with God in knowledge is not a mere affair of some one department of knowledge called religious, although it is now for the most part carried on departmentally. Although men separate off for their practical convenience the study of plants from the study of animals, and a specialist may separate off the egg of the newt and study nothing else, and even think, at least seriously, of nothing else; although we may not only speak of religion, or knowledge, or philosophy as separate one from another but act as though they were, yet if the Christian and the philosopher and the scientific man are right in holding that there is a unity in the multiplicity of things, a 'uniformity of nature,' an 'Absolute,' or 'One God,' then religion and science and philosophy are only separated, if separate at all, by an artifice or a convention. You cannot really *separate* knowing, in a man's activity, from his feeling and acting, nor his feeling from acting and knowing, nor his acting from knowing and feeling, nor his activity from himself; although you can *distinguish* each from the others. They are different, but their difference is embraced within a oneness. So it is with religion and science and philosophy. They are all results of man's activity in relation to a reality of innumerable aspects and unfathomable depth; and they may all be means by which he ascends the ladder of his experience of God.

Therefore the Christian does his own sacramental and incarnational principles a grave injustice if and when he tries to turn away from science and philosophy. Not only this— he cannot really do it. When he succeeds in turning away from that which he believes to be all there is of science and philosophy, he does not cut out from his creed and his theology the science and philosophy incorporated in them— a science and a philosophy which undoubtedly need correction that they may move and grow with the movement and the growth of experience. It is only the science and philosophy grown to new ripeness and new truth since the day when the great bulk of his Christian tradition was laid down in written words to be transmitted to him, that as a matter of fact he is rejecting. And he is able to reject these just and only because he has already in this tradition such science and philosophy as serves to make for him some sort of a *Weltanschauung*, a world-picture, you may say. It is useless to protest that a man can be religious without having a world-picture; he cannot even be a man without one. And the only question for him is whether it shall or shall not be as wide in its extent and as good as he can make it, whether he shall or shall not include within it all the knowledge and vision of God he might include.

Plainly—that is, plainly to the Christian—if the scientific man or the philosopher does not include in his view of the world what the Christian knows and sees, he is the loser. His picture is not all it might be. But the same, *mutatis mutandis*, is true of the Christian. For all is God's and of God. And if we never before discovered this, we see it when we discover the point where science and religion meet, where the scientific knowledge of the world passes into the sacramental, and the scientific knowledge of man, as part of the world, passes into the incarnational; each to be crowned there, each to be interpreted and fulfilled.

To this discovery there is only one theoretic obstacle which is insuperable. It is the acceptance of mechanism as a root-principle in either science or religion. I say nothing of philosophy, because there is now-a-days no mechanistic philosophy (that is, no materialistic philosophy) that need be feared. But in science and in religion mechanism is still a danger, and the acceptance of it as the fundamental principle of working and construction in a world-picture is an obstacle that cannot be passed. There is nothing to be done except to overturn it.

In regard to science much (as we have seen) has already been done; more is being done. How is it in regard to religion? What about mechanism there?

CHAPTER III
The religions of all nations are derived from each
nation's different reception of the poetic genius,
which is everywhere called the spirit of prophecy.
Blake.

The Christian has not escaped the dangers of the common
lot. He too, despite his own contrary principles, has, from the
beginning of the Christian Church, been tempted as we all
are to trust to mechanism and even to sacrifice in its favour
the powers of life. We ought not to be surprised; what else
can reasonably be expected? A good machine, whether it be
made of steel and brass, or of language, or of settled
formulae and plans, or of any other product of life, is an
admirable servant. It is convenient; it brings satisfaction to
widespread and deeply-rooted needs of life itself. Moreover
there is nothing mysterious (so it seems), or even
problematic, about it. The plain man is not called upon to
question or wonder or speculate in regard to anything behind
it, any powers or vague connexions with powers, not
understood. The good machine does what it has to do and
there's an end of it. A man knows where he is when he has
such a thing—or when it has him. There is even a sense of
comfort and security in being ruled and cared for by it, as,
for example, in the case of the machinery of a State.

In this difficult world there seems, indeed there is, need for
something of the kind to supply a considerable part of our
religious demand. We are social beings; we are, as we are
beginning to see more plainly, brothers in a community; we
must organize our religion as we organize everything else in
which the community of persons has its common interest.
And God, the Christian may say, and has said, would not
leave us, has not left us, to uncertainty and to our questioning
and wondering and speculative adventure. He has provided
answers to our questions, facts in response to our wondering,

an open view for our speculation. Or, to put it in another way, he has given us a 'plan' or 'scheme,' or an ecclesiastical apparatus, of salvation; he has revealed religious truth to us and marked out an established method of approaching him and securing our own safety in respect of his judgement and our destiny at his hands. Nothing of so great importance has been left, could have been left, in the hands of men, to find out or not find out—poor creatures that we are.

Now, there is truth behind this, both as to the part of God and as to the part of man in the matter. We are social, we are brethren, we must organize. God, so all Christians say and many philosophers, no more leaves us to ourselves than he leaves to itself any part of his worlds. But Christians formally declare in their Creed that he is no machine-maker; he is Lord and Giver of Life. They complain, too, against science on the ground that (as they have come to believe) it must of its constant character set material mechanism above life in the order of the world. They are pledged to oppose this; and when they complain against science for a fault and failure which is soon—so many biologists and philosophers declare—to be a fault and a failure of the past, they are faithful to their pledge. But they are men, with the faults and failures of men. Habit has its snares for them; the complication of needs that meets them in their effort to maintain themselves, body, mind and spirit, in the world, entangles them. The short cut, the provided means, everything and anything that seems to make matters easy or safe—in short, the logical or legalistic or institutional machine—is attractive. And for most men this machine in any of its protean forms, is perhaps only the more attractive the more valued is the treasure it seems to ensure or to protect. The faith once for all delivered—how precious that is! Salvation in this world and the next—can anything be of greater import for man? Let us make these things secure, whatever else we risk. Only fools or the reckless would embrace chances of adventure where so much is at stake.

So, in spite of the Christian avowal of the superiority and the supremacy of life over its instruments, Christianity has everywhere given disastrous place to the letter and the tool.

Against this the first prophet and the last, in every religion, must always protest. It is the enemy of enemies for all prophets. You can see war waged against it in the Old Testament; you can see that war carried to the utmost in the Gospel of the New. Now the challenge rings among us more clearly than it has rung for this long time. And, as ever, it has new notes and a new phrasing of its music.... That, perhaps, is why so many of us fail to recognize it for what it is. That, certainly, is why the due honour paid to prophets of the past does not prevent men from stoning or neglecting those of the present. The voice is always different, because it is the voice of life.

The use and need for the prophet is a fact not only in religion but in all the arts and in philosophy. He alone keeps any one of these in touch with life, or rather recalls it to life when it has been encumbered or perhaps even arrested by that which life has made. He is, in very deed, the voice of the encumbered spirit making itself heard, proclaiming in one fashion or another that the pursuit of beauty and truth as well as of holiness is of the spirit, and must have the spirit's liberty or it will altogether fail. In the arts and in philosophy we do not call him a prophet, but often, in the arts, we speak of him (when we have recovered from the shock he gives) as 'inspired,' and in philosophy we call him 'great.' Great he is and inspired—we could hardly choose better and more deeply significant words. He is the enlarger of life and the bearer of the spirit, whether he uses the language of philosophy, of poetry, painting or music, or of religion. But always he comes waging war upon our superstitious devotion to the things that have once been made, proclaiming either divine truth or divine beauty or divine holiness (according to his mission), as that for the sake of which they must ever be remade.

We who have learnt our lesson from science as well as from philosophy should be sure friends to the prophet. We have learnt enough of the story of life to see that from its beginning on the earth it strove towards liberty, towards the indetermination by circumstance and the freedom of choice that man has reached. We have seen life lost in mere material size and crushed by the weight of material protective armour; and we know what these things mean. We know, too, what entanglement in habit means for our own selves. We are good and sure friends of the prophet. Or we may be, if we will.

It is high time that he should find such friends—men ready to meet him with that in their minds which prepares his way before him. He has too long been the voice driven to cry in the wilderness. Too long and too often he has found men opposing him with a settled prejudice in favour of the vested interests—the sanctified, it may be, and glorified vested interests—of law and order and creed, of institution and crystallized opinion. It is time that a new atmosphere should be made about him and that these things should be visibly set in their right place and held at their right value. When this is done the secret materialism of his opponents will be brought to light. For, however it may be disguised, all overvaluing of the instrumental product of life's activity comes of the undue depreciation of living spirit and the undue appreciation of its means. Science and philosophy, in teaching us now to seek for the true relation of matter and spirit, are also teaching us to lend a willing ear to the prophet. When we have learnt to see in man the beginning of a synthesis of order and freedom in a vital harmony not manifest in those starry heavens to which men point as the standing witness of God against prophets of new freedom, we are ready to confess, if we have found our God, that in him that perfect synthesis is declared and in man it is foreshadowed and to be pursued.

CHAPTER IV

Hearken to me, ye children of the Immortal,
dwellers of the heavenly worlds, I have known the
Supreme Person who comes as light from the dark
beyond.
Isha Upanishat.

Studying at its best the Christian view of the world of life—
and it is not worth any man's while to study it at less—we
find that Jesus Christ stands there always as greatest among
prophets, though 'more than a prophet.' He is in the line of
the prophets but at their head; he is their culmination and
their fulfilment. He knew himself to be a prophet, and to
have the lot of one who 'is not without honour save in his
own country.' He lived and taught, and he and his teaching
were received, after the manner of the prophets that had gone
before. Like Isaiah and Jeremiah he spoke the language of
drama and poetry, and gave body in parable and pictorial
visions to his message. Like them he spoke and preached
always with passion and as being conscious of a very wall of
opposing forces. For him as for them the exaltation of
religious machinery above religious life, and all self-
satisfaction through mere forms and ceremonies, meant an
onset of spiritual death. To use these things as a shelter
within which a man might follow his self-seeking bent,
whether of greed or of fear, was the worst (but one) of sins.
'Hypocrites,' that is, 'play-actors', 'generation of vipers,' he
said of the professionally religious of his time. That there
was for him one sin greater than such play-acting is of his
own supreme greatness. No other prophet recognized and
denounced as he did the sin that cannot be forgiven; for no
other prophet had as he had the full personally realized
revelation of an indwelling God whom man, consciously,
might cast out. This, with his marvellous balance of
judgement in regard to the letter or the machine and the
spirit—the organ and the life that shapes and uses it—is a

marked element in his *differentia* among prophets. And we, who are friends to them all in so far as they protest against depreciation of spirit and life, and against men who make of the products of life from which life has departed obstacles to the urgency of the present, have to consider whether we can go with him as far as he goes, or whether this element of difference between him and the rest is in any way to weaken our alliance with him. He is not only one among his fellows; he is also unquestionably different from them. Is there anything about this difference that should make us who are friends of the prophets quarrel with the Christian who accepts and welcomes it?

First, let us look at his attitude towards the instruments of religion as compared and contrasted with that of other prophets of his race. *'Your new moons and your appointed feasts my soul hateth,'*—that is the note of the elder prophets. *'The Sabbath was made for man, not man for the Sabbath'*— that is his. The prophet of old was contemptuous of institutional and ceremonial religion; he suffered, as we say, from reaction and went to extremes, reprobating the instrument as well as the spirit that misinterpreted and misused it. Jesus taught in the synagogue, cleansed the temple from those who had made the historic house of prayer to be a den of thieves, sent the leper to show himself to the priest, and in general accepted the institutions of religion, and the hierarchical organization, of the place and people that were his own. Yet no man can say he overvalued these. His insistence on the spiritual freedom of man and the pre-eminence of spirit and life was both constant and passionate. The institution he accepted, as he accepted the tools of his carpenter's trade, the food and furniture of life as he found it, the language and the manners of his people. Freedom and unity, love, truth, beauty and holiness, as realities in the life of God and man, for these he pleaded, preached, worked, suffered and died. Yet those other things were not to be despised or left undone. He came and he lived not to destroy but to fulfil. In this he is pre-eminent among, apart from, the religious prophets who went before him. His piercing and balanced judgement was the primary source of Christian sacramentalism. He despised nothing of the earth and the body; he found a place for all in the life of the spirit. He was the first preacher to point to loveliness in the flowers of the field; and for twelve hundred years no other, in any nation or kind of religion, did the like. Then Francis of Assisi, his true follower, sang the Song of the Sun. The long history of Christian sacramentalism spreads out far and deep and gathers up in itself from all quarters the pursuit of beauty is well as the hunger and thirst after righteousness and truth; but its pure source is plain to see in the Gospels. There the fine adjustment of the relation between matter and spirit, life and its organs, is maintained. There the value and the meaning and pertinence of life's own instruments to its user, of the body to the soul, is as clearly insisted on as is the supremacy in both meaning and value of life itself. There is none of the abstract spiritualism that is one of the prophet's most dangerous snares. There is none of the contempt and the blinding reaction which so often disfigure and discredit his utterances. And for this, we who have come fresh from learning our new lesson about the movement of organic life and its difficult striving upon the earth may dare to praise him. It is a beginning for us. Not in this respect, at least, shall we stand aloof from him or complain that science or philosophy has built a barrier against him. That Christians the world over have lost touch with him in this regard as in others is for the moment nothing to us. We know that they are feeble and fallible like ourselves and that his way of judgement is hard. To keep the balance even, never to allow a secret materialism to be brought into the scale, or a protest to sink into repudiation—this is hard indeed. And we know that a thousand other temptations have beset the Christian during the centuries that have gone by and that, being as he is and just as we are ourselves, he has succumbed to not a few of them. We know all that; but we are seeking to find out what greatness it is that lies behind all the faults and follies, the absurdities, the crimes even, of Christians, and keeps Christianity alive and potent. We begin to see, perhaps, that this greatness is Christ—that it is 'Jesus the prophet of Nazareth in Galilee.'

Of this greatness and its character he himself had an unique consciousness which was a most important and most marked element in his difference from the Hebrew prophets before him. He 'spoke with authority and not as the Scribes,' not as those theologians and jurists whose strength rested on tradition and the letter of the past; he spoke, in short, as a prophet. So the people discovered. The voice of the prophets was characteristically authoritative and neither showed respect for tradition nor claimed its support. But the note of the prophets of old was '*Thus saith the Lord*'; and the note of the prophet of Nazareth was '*I say unto you*.' Both came among men with an authority lacking to the followers of tradition; but by the first it was thought of as delegated, in the second it was recognized as inherent. Not, '*the Lord said unto me*,' but '*I say unto you*.' The difference is enormous; it is also profound in significance and implications. It means, to begin with, a different knowledge of God. No longer is God only speaking to his messengers across a dividing space, speaking as a king upon his throne might to a subject at his feet, charging that subject with a mission. The message is no longer carried and reported by a man; it is originated in him and given by him. Jesus is conscious that the life and spirit of God are become his own life and spirit. He knows the indwelling God given to be made man in co-operative union with man, knows him in and through and as himself, the prophet of Nazareth in Galilee. He does not need to refer either to a God, or to a tradition, that is extraneous to himself. Therefore his prophetic authority exceeds not only that of the

Scribes but that of all the prophets. It gave this impression to those of his contemporaries who had eyes to see and ears to hear. To such men it gives the same impression now. And if there are Christians who explain the impression and reason from it, erroneously, have we any right to be surprised? Consider the height to which we have been carried and the problems that open up before us as we survey this man. Consider the habits of interpretation most usual among us. Consider the tangibility and conspicuousness of *things*, the intangibility and, to the senses and the mind itself, the elusive mysteries of personality, of nature, of consciousness, even of knowledge and every other manifest activity. We cannot fairly blame Christians for what has been done among them in an attempt to explain and reason about Jesus Christ. The attempt has been honest enough and successful enough to hold the allegiance of thinking men for generations.

The truth is that we are learning, as we never learnt before, to question the manner of our own thinking about these high matters. We have become aware, as we were not, of the insidious materialism of our instruments of thought. We have learnt that to apply a logic of things and their qualities to problems of the nature of God and man is to ensure misunderstanding. So when Christians tell us that the person of Jesus Christ is divine and that he had, or was, or is, a human nature and a divine nature, and a human will and a divine will conjoined in the divine person, we see plainly that they are applying to the truth of him that logic of things and their qualities which they have acquired through dealing easily and habitually with things. They are trying to explain him by taking human nature as one thing or set of qualities, and divine nature as another, and they are joining them by a third. You see two vertical stones and one across the top. And if the stones are alive and the top one 'hypostatically' effects the union between the other two, stones they still are; or sets of qualities conceived as things, which is all the same.

The mighty consciousness of Jesus escaped entanglement by these logical, spatial, materialistic nets. He knew by experience the activity of a will in which the will of God and the will of man were united and engaged at once in one purpose. He knew, felt, lived, God and man as one in himself. And in the fulness of this he differed from all other prophets, for whom it was at best, and that but rarely, an unrealized ideal.

Shall we say, then, that for us and for Christians it is well not to reason about the problems he presents to thought? Even if we do, we shall reason and so will they. Neither we nor they can help it. But we may put our reasoning together, and learn each from the other. There is a meeting-place here, inviting us to join hands.

CHAPTER V

*Where Love is the Lover, Love streaming from
the Lover is the Lover; the Lover streaming from
himself, and existing in another Person.
Traherne.*

Aut Deus aut homo non bonus—so Christians have said and
believed. The dilemma, though comfortable for not a few
among them, and having about it a certain truth, often
involves a false conception of both man and God. The truth
it holds is not their comfort; they do not know that. What
most people mean when they use the dilemma is that the
prophet of Nazareth was either as a person God and not as a
person man, or he was as a person man and a bad one. It
seems conclusive, this either-or. But there is no logical
weapon more fatal to our discovery of the truth of spirit and
life. 'Either-or' comes from a field of interest where things
stand out conspicuous and apart, and cannot be thought of as
communicating virtue and riches and themselves one to
another. It brings with it an insinuating suggestion, if not
assertion, that the affairs of spirit and life are in the same
case. Personality, which is an affair of spirit and life, seems
no more to admit of such intercommunication than does
materiality. Two persons can no more communicate
themselves to each other than two stones. Which, on the
crude exposed face of it, is nonsense. They can, they do; and
we know it.

Unquestionably the great prophet spoke with the authority
which lesser prophets attributed to God. He made claims,
very high claims. Was he only an arrogant and blasphemous
man? (He might, perhaps, have been deluded, though the
dilemma ignores that possibility—as well it may.) Or was he
God? There is no half-way house of vital identity between
man as person and God as person, any more than there is a
half-way house of material identity between a diamond and

a pebble off the beach. *Either-or.* So this dilemma goes. It is very simple, all too simple. It applies beautifully to pebbles and diamonds; why not to living persons? Particularly and excellently, why not to man and God?

Now, as a matter of fact, I am trying to communicate to you at this very moment something that is mine. My knowledge (or my ignorant opinion) is written down on the paper before you, and you will or may receive it—to do with it what you choose. Henceforth it is, or may be, yours as well as mine. Again, I try to communicate to you the content of my will for you. You know and feel that I want your will to be brought to coincide with mine, so that my will and yours shall be vitally identical in regard to what I am writing about. In some degree or another you and I may become one in this regard. I shall then have communicated my knowledge (or my ignorant opinion) and my will to you and they will to some extent or another be both yours and mine. This communication and co-operation is a matter of our choosing to enter into it and be and work together. We have it in our own hands. It is quite different from the relation we have to each other as being parts in the universe, or elements in God looked upon as the pantheist looks upon him, which makes him no more than the universe. We can't help that relation. We share it with the stones as well as with each other and with God. It is a purely abstract business and belongs to 'the night in which all cows are black.' Our cows, on the other hand, are of every sort of colour; and we find, we actually do find, that we can pass on our colours to each other, dye the different cow to our tinge and in turn be dyed. We are concrete, not abstract; and our vital identity one with another is concrete too. It may be and might not be. We choose whether it shall be or not. And, happily, we choose that it shall be, up to a point, far more often and more steadily than we choose that it shall not. Hence the existence of a human community in common knowledge and reason and common will—up to a point.

I give you here in these pages, or at least proffer you, as I have said, 'something of mine.' That is what it looks like. But, enquiring further, I ask whether as a matter of fact 'I' am separate from 'something of mine,' as, let us say an engine is separate from the power it produces and the work it does. Do I produce thought and knowledge as an engine produces so much horse-power? Is my will or my reason a sort of thing that produces activity as a flower produces its scent? The scent is not the flower; the horse-power is not the engine. There is always a producing *thing* behind such products. Is there a producing thing behind my knowledge and activity? And the only reasonable answer we can give to this question is that there is not. In my spirit and life there is nothing in the least like a thing or a machine; and when we reason about spirit and life as though there were we plunge into a very sea of confusion. My reason and my will *are* myself. I am not a thing and I do not produce like a thing. I give and I communicate my very self in giving and communicating my knowledge, my purpose, my will. And in so far as you receive these and take them into yourself you receive me— spirit and life—as person. By harmony between us our wills and reason, our selves, coalesce; they become identical in the concrete, vital identity peculiar to persons, impossible to things, and dependent for its maintenance on the maintenance of harmony by their own free activity. Very partial it is, no doubt, seen by all of us 'as in a mirror darkly'; but it points, with a finger that should draw all eyes, to a great fulfilment. That fulfilment is 'the goal, not the starting-point of human endeavour.' The blank identity of co-existence in a universe is, you may say, a starting-point for reflexion; but real concrete mental coalescence between each and all of us is a real concrete starting-point of life in a personal world. The goal lies far ahead, where that union of persons foreshadowed in our fragmentary intercourse and the low beginnings of our community of life shall be won through that which alone can give it, our union and communion with God. This is more or less a philosopher's way of putting the matter; but it means the same as the Christian's.

Now there is a question that forces itself upon us here. Can there be a coalescence of mind and will, an identity, between God and man, of this living, spiritual—that is, real, concrete—kind? Or is God so different from man as to be incommunicable to him? Is he remote from man in his own nature or, indeed, not only remote but alien? The answer to this is that if he is even remote, not to say alien, he is nothing to us and we may ignore him.

The Christian's God certainly is not remote; he is all men's lover and father and they are all his beloved and his sons. The philosopher's God is sometimes made blankly, abstractly, identical with us, and then we may ignore him; because a blank identity simply is, as conceived in thought, and like the alien God it means nothing for us. But more often nowadays the philosopher's God is like the Christian's in that he both transcends his universe and indwells it; for the philosopher has begun in good earnest to reckon with life and with science and human experience at large. God indwelt Jesus Christ, and he knew God as lover and father both. He spoke as though God had communicated himself to him in a fulness we do not know among ourselves. There was an identity of will, it seems, recognized by him, between himself and God, and an identity of reason and knowledge. And if God is Spirit and Lord and Giver of life, then, if the prophet was right, in this identity by fulness of communication, this personal coalescence of reason and will, God, very God, gave himself to very man, and very man entered into personal union with very God. The transcendent

God indwelt the man, was immanent within him as the man's own self; and the man's own self was lifted up into the self of God. The intercommunication of person with person, which we see as the prerogative of persons, was complete.

We have confessed this to be the goal of human endeavour; let us allow ourselves to think that in regard to us it may be the goal, also, of divine endeavour, and that in the man who offered no opposition to God it was attained. As long as we do not indulge in the secret materialism of regarding a person as a thing *producing* knowledge or activity, instead of as *being* that knowledge and activity, we shall have no difficulty in recognizing the fact that where knowledge and will in two persons coincide, there also the persons coincide. We shall be able to see that a man is identical with God, in the only sense identity can have for personal beings, when he fully knows the mind of God and his will is bent on the same ends as the will of God. Then this man is both man and God in one, for God indwells him by that activity which he truly is.

If we object, as we frequently do, that no man can fully know the mind of God, we must tell ourselves that if a man knows the essential, permanently valuable truth of life which wise men have ever sought as wisdom, then all that is worth while in knowledge, all that upon which parts and kinds of 'knowledges' must be built up, is his, included within his *Weltanschauung*, his living view of the world. The principle, the ground, of all truth, and therefore of all knowledge, he knows and has.

We think of the writer of the Fourth Gospel giving us, as a prayer of Jesus, the aspiration that 'they all may be one, as thou, Father, art in me and I in thee, that they also may be one in us.' He has the goal of our endeavour in plain sight; he must have felt that impulse of the spirit towards it which is not exhausted, never can be exhausted, by any one man.

CHAPTER VI

Thy judgment is in the mute pain of sleepless love;
In the blush of pure hearts;
In the tears of the night of desolation;
In the pale morning-light of forgiveness.
Rabindranath Tagore.

We are going far with the Christian. Life is indeed a bond; it is materialism that divides the seekers after truth. The secret materialism of the Christian and his trust in religious machinery must bring him into conflict with those who put their trust in other kinds of machines. We who are trusting life, and are trying not to interpret it in terms of the logic of things, find ourselves side by side with those Christians faithful enough to their supreme leader and their own principles to do the same. So we may walk willingly with them and hear what they have to say in more intimate talk than there can be when the spirit of community is wanting.

In this matter of personality and its self-communicating power they have been beforehand with us, as in so many other matters. Jesus has been for them a fountain of wisdom and insight, and while they have kept close to him his wisdom and his insight have been-imparted to them. He has been in them a well-spring wanting to the negligent world. 'Whosoever drinketh of the water that I shall give him,' the disciple hears him say, 'shall never thirst; but the water that I shall give him shall be in him a well of water springing up into everlasting life.' That is what it means to be indwelt by God, 'the fountain of living waters,' as the older prophet calls him. And we think of what we have learnt about personality and the inseparability of the spirit from its own content of knowledge and volition, of love, too, and righteousness, and joy in beauty and truth. We think of the intercommunication of man with man and of men with God and his 'Christ'—that is, the man 'whose individuality,' as a Christian philosopher says, 'is identified with God in the unity of all his thought and action with the divine knowledge and the divine purpose.' All these come to mind when we hear of a fountain of living waters becoming a well-spring for those who drink of it.

But it may be that we turn away with a sigh from such intimate talk, knowing how far we are ourselves from the union with God which the Christian depicts. And it may be, too, that there dawns upon us the thought that when this Christian speaks of 'atonement' he means, most likely, some process of God by which that union is accomplished, and the neglect or opposition of men is overcome. What difference is there, we may be inclined to ask, between divine incarnation, as the Christian sees it,—God's communication of himself, the fountain of living waters, to men—and an atonement between him and them? Is not the union of incarnation the very act and process of atonement? Is not the redemption of man effected in and through the self-expression of God in him? When he is one with God he is 'redeemed' from the neglect and opposition of sin, and of the rejection of God; and then God is manifest and expressed in him. Is this a question of words? Perhaps, rather, it is a question of emphasis on one or other side, man's side or God's.

But if, for the moment, we lay emphasis on the side of man and speak of atonement and redemption instead of speaking of incarnation and our communion and union with God, there are certainly elements of special difficulty to be encountered. The explanations of Christians are by no means as trustworthy as their insight and the knowledge they derive from their great 'Redeemer.' They explain in legalistic terms, or materialistic, or in terms of a despotic rule, a process and an act of life given and received. They are prone to ignore the prophet in favour of the Scribe or the Pharisee. And once again the prophet may justly put into the mouth of God the old reproach—'My people have committed two evils; they have forsaken me, the fountain of living waters, and hewed them out cisterns, broken cisterns, that can hold no water.' They build up their inventions and hide beneath them the sublimity of living fact; and we who ask them concerning the fact are shown the ruins of those inventions. We ask them for bread and they give us the stones they have put together. There is hardly a religious problem or question, or fact and process, more encumbered than this with that tradition which makes the word of God of none effect. No doubt there are Christians who are both able and willing to help such men and women as are likely to ask their help; the difficulty is to find such Christians. Let us see, now, how we can work out for ourselves an understanding of what is really meant by atonement between men and God, what Christians really mean when they express themselves so ill about it, what it really is that really happens.

Atonement between God and men undoubtedly implies the forgiveness of sinful men by God. They cannot possibly enter into union with him unless they are forgiven. When they sin against their fellow-men they cannot be united or re-united with them on any other condition than that their fellows forgive them. But, we must insist, it is immoral to forgive them unless they at least *will* to cast away their sinfulness. It is always immoral, too, not to punish, that is, not to condemn, sin and sinfulness; and therefore (since a man and his activity are one) the sinner. How then can God at once condemn (or punish) and forgive the sin, sinfulness and the sinner? Are not condemnation (or punishment) and forgiveness mutually exclusive? If we condemn or punish do we not fail to forgive? If we forgive, must we not remit punishment and cease to condemn?

Now here is a difficulty that reflexion should remove. For it comes of what happens in the lower stages of man's social relations and spiritual growth. We think of punishment as somehow the expression of vindictiveness, while forgiveness alone is the expression of love. So it is in us beginners. So it begins to cease to be, even in us, as we grow into new life and a new spirit. Let us think how we should behave to an evil-doer if we loved him to the utmost of our power of love. Should we condone his evil-doing by withholding that condemnation which is expressed in punishment, whether of look or word or deed (as circumstance demands), and extend to him an artifice of forgiveness in which the moral disunion between him and ourselves shall be concealed? Would that truly represent our faithful love for him, that love which must seek not an appearance but a reality of harmony, and for his sake tolerate no encouragement, not even the slightest possibility of deriving encouragement, for his evil doing? Obviously it would not. For his sake we should unmistakably condemn, making known to him in look or word or deed our condemnation. It would be the expression of our love and, with forgiveness, is of the nature and property of love. We should feel no shadow of vindictiveness. In our relation with him the forgiveness and the condemnation of love would be one.

We encounter here a false antithesis in a matter of spirit and life. Forgiveness and punishment in God or in the man of God can neither be antithetical nor need to be reconciled. In the life of love they are not divided. God, who is love as he is spirit and life, forgives and condemns by one consistent act of love. There is no immoral condonation in his forgiveness, no vindictiveness about his punishment. And this the Christian knows both by his own experience and by the life and lessons of his redeeming Lord. 'Whom the Lord loveth he chasteneth, and scourgeth every son whom he receiveth.' No true Christian would have it otherwise.

'If forgiveness means—as it properly does—the wise and patient care for the criminal's welfare, for his regeneration and recovery into the life of a good society, then there is no distinction whatever between forgiveness and punishment.' That, precisely, is what forgiveness ought to be made to mean, and punishment likewise. But again we see in a mirror darkly and are confused by our history and our own shortcomings. Therefore even Christians misjudge God, or make for themselves 'broken cisterns'—a false God who is no fountain of living waters, pouring forth a never-failing, self-consistent, self-giving love; but a judge, a king, a despot, after the pattern of the world, a God aloof administering punishment or forgiveness, both alike unworthy and misplaced. There is no difficulty at all in this question of punishment and forgiveness if we remember perfect love and its aim, as Jesus shows them.

Moreover, we must bear in mind, nothing about God who 'is spirit' is either an artifice or a machine. So his punishments, his expressed condemnations, are never artificial, never mechanical. They arise 'naturally,' as we say; and in large part we provide them, we men, ourselves. There are certain 'natural' consequences, miscalled punishments, which are entailed upon the body as, for instance, when a child puts his hand into the fire or a man disregards what we call the 'laws' of health. The due and true moral punishment of persons by persons is just as natural. The nature of persons is spiritual in the order of their uplifted life, and is one with that life. Their nature is, in fact, no other than that life and those persons. We cannot separate, though we may sometimes in word distinguish, between the man and his nature. Consequently all due and right punishment by persons (punishment by love, which is the same as forgiveness by love) is wholly natural. It is a natural consequence of sin, the reaction against sin with which good persons or a good society must encounter it. There is no arbitrary infliction of punishment, and no arbitrary forgiveness, by the good man, the good society, or the good God. Nor should there be in regard to his own sins or sinfulness by the man who newly rejects them, the newly penitent man. He, the new man, reacts according to his new nature, and in one and the same activity should condemn and forgive himself. He must be penitent but he should not be remorseful. If he does not forgive himself as well as condemn himself, it may be because he is not humble enough and penitent enough to bear with the fact that he has deserved his condemnation.

We must remind ourselves, however, that it is of spiritual nature in ourselves to *choose*. The activity of love is chosen and determined by the good man, with its forgiveness and its punishment. And although the perfection of God must preclude choice between alternatives, although for perfect wisdom there can never be more than one course open, yet there is no automatism, there cannot be automatism of the mechanical kind, in God who, as the Christian maintains, *is* love. His love is willed though not chosen. It is of the vital, intelligent, voluntary activity of a spiritual being. And so both punishment and forgiveness are willed, in God or in man; and as the man approaches full union with God so does his choice approach that inevitable wisdom for which there is no longer consciousness of choice. This is the manner of spirit and life; that which is personally real in any man, all that is in God, is not merely consented to or assented to but is always actively willed, never compulsorily or mechanically apportioned. So it is right and reasonable to say that God or the man of God punishes and forgives. It is not right to say that the punishment and forgiveness of either, though it is wholly natural, is in any kind of way automatic with the automatism of a machine, or even with that relative automatism of material things which we speak of as natural law. Without the activity of love there can be no true punishment and no true forgiveness; there is only vindictiveness or condonation.

The treatment we have given our wrong-doers in the past is not fitted to throw clear light on Christian atonement and the ways of God with man. On the contrary, it has obscured both. But we are learning. Truth, experience, and the *Gesta Christi* work for our learning. Or, as the Christian says, the divine spirit works for it and 'strives' with us, that is, works with us that we may work out our own salvation.

We have begun to say to the children we are training— 'Come now, this is *wrong*; let's see how we' [*we*, mark you] 'can set it right.' We have discovered that unless the child works with us our punishment fails, and our forgiveness fails, of any real effect for goodness. But Christians knew this from their beginning, though many of them forget they did. In the last resort it is why Christ died.

When, carrying with us our new method, we have passed from the child to the criminal, and extend to him that 'wise and patient care' for his welfare, which is forgiveness and punishment in one, we shall be in a better position for seeing what Christian atonement really means and is—how real it is and how it depends on co-operation between the Saviour and the offender; how, always, the Saviour must win the offender first if he is to save him. Then we shall read the Gospels of the Christian with new eyes and a new understanding.

If you want to see punishment and forgiveness both in one, turn to the parable of the prodigal son. Could any punishment be more salutary or more piercing to the man whose penitence had shown him his utter unworthiness?

Could forgiveness be more complete, more gracious, than that which he received? Consider how his penitence must have been deepened, and his sense of unworthiness increased, when he found himself in his father's arms, and his father's house, honoured, rejoiced over, feasted? In proportion to the depth and fulness of penitence do these two, punishment and forgiveness, given in love, become distinguishable only by the reaction to them of the penitent. He alone knows how love hurts and heals in one and the same act and moment.

Then, if you want to learn the many forms punishment may take, seek further. Look at the story of the woman taken in adultery. 'Hath no man condemned thee?' ... 'Neither do I condemn thee: go, and *sin no more.*' Punishment and forgiveness imparted in one profound paradox of love's judgement. What do you think was its effect on the woman who had looked into the prophet's eyes as he lifted them from the dust? 'Hath no man condemned thee?' 'No man, Lord,' she said; and they were the words humility and shame would choose.

A degree further—consider the picture of a final judgement, with the 'Son of man in his glory' and the nations gathered before him to be shown their union with him, or their disunion, in a clearness none could mistake. 'Come, ye blessed,' he says, 'inherit the kingdom prepared for you from the foundation of the world'—the kingdom in which all men are one with the Holiest, with the living Truth himself and Beauty 'in his glory'—come with me. For I was an hungred, thirsty, a stranger.... Naked and ye clothed me, sick, in prison, and ye came unto me.... And yet these blessed had never known what they did. It was not he, so far as they knew, that they had succoured. Not for his sake but for love's they had done it; not even, indeed, at the heart of it, for love's sake, but because they loved, because in them the well-spring of love streamed forth and they gave their very selves to those others who had only need of them. They were of love and were love's own. Love as shown to these who needed it was not distinguishable, even by their reaction to it, into punishment and forgiveness. It was but love.

Then those others—'Depart from me,' he says—and there was a vision painted of the unutterable horrors of a state of separation and loneliness and self-embittered remorse—'I was an hungred and ye gave me no meat.' They also, had not known—'Lord, when saw we thee an hungred?' If they had known they would assuredly have hastened to him with their meat, asked him to their feasts, lavished all upon him. But for what sake? For no other than their own. Love had no place in their hearts, nor had the Lord. Only self-seeking. They were their own Lords and Gods. And thenceforth they had to know it. In their impenitent, disappointed, cheated (they would say) and remorseful hearts there was no room for anything but the sense of punishment. Their inevitable reaction to the voice of love, as it reproached their lack of love, shut out both forgiveness and all possibility of the sense of it.

So we come to the extreme of distinction between the ways of the showing of love. Here is all punishment, it seems, to the sinner. But it is he who makes love so. It is very love that punishes, a consistent, unwavering love which, in the sinner's last extremity, shows itself to the utmost he can receive and in the only way he can receive. What, I ask you, would a man like this make of a love that should express itself (if in the nature of love it could thus express itself) as condoning the want of love and professing oneness in so complete an alienation? Not only does the nature of love forbid such an expression, but the nature of the self-worshipper, who cannot receive it.

There is a very marvellous knowledge of the hidden heart shown in these prophetic teachings. As we converse with the Supreme Person of the Gospels we feel him searching out our bones and marrow. To him there lies open the secret of disunion among us personal beings and the secret of the utmost furtherance, and the means towards furtherance, of the conversion of our will from self-seeking to love-finding. This utmost furtherance necessarily falls short of the compulsion love can never even contemplate or man endure. A man compelled to love is unthinkable. Words, mere empty words these are that so speak of him. He cannot be. If he could be compelled he could not be man; if the semblance of love were forced upon him it would not be love. But the atonement in which the Christian believes shows the love of God working to further love in man to an utmost God alone can reach. Punishment and forgiveness work together as that love, and the life of Jesus and the Cross on which he died are at once their final showing-forth, their clearest call to man, and the tremendous acceptance by man of all that they entail and are.

Here, indeed, is the fountain of love in its fulness. We need not wonder that the disciple, having in mind his living and triumphant Lord, hears him say to us who desire to drink of the waters of love—'Whosoever drinketh of the water that I shall give him shall never thirst; but the water that I shall give him shall be in him a well of water springing up into everlasting life.'

Christian atonement means restoration to the only real and full union and communion of persons, that of divine love.

CHAPTER VII

Nature, in a fashion whose details are still only
faintly hinted to us men, constitutes a vast society.
Royce.

The Christian shows in his root principles, we are bound to confess, a profound sense of personality and of the relations of persons. That this comes of his relation to the Supreme Person from whom he has derived them can hardly be denied. It is in a person, Jesus Christ, that he has seen God and learnt about him; and the judgements and love of God that he discerns he discerns in Christ. As the spirit of Christ becomes one with his spirit so do his own judgements and his own love become those of God in him, and his principles are embodied in his life. All wisdom is divine, and all love, the Christian says. And, undoubtedly, men who are earnestly and disinterestedly seeking these, and discovering how in that search they penetrate into the truth and reality of moral and practical affairs of life, must find that the Christian is worth listening to, perhaps even worth watching. That is, when he has 'the mind of Christ.' Otherwise he confuses judgement and blurs, if he does not efface, his principles. In 'the mind of Christ' he is for us 'a well-spring of water'; without that, if he only calls himself by the name and is either the Scribe, the Pharisee, or the false prophet, he is far more helpless, far more misleading and misled, than they are who honestly seek truth and know they have not found it.

In the last chapter we heard what the man with the mind of Christ had to say about punishment and forgiveness as between persons. And one difficulty that disturbs others, many others, besides those who approach the Christian religion from the direction of science, has surely been lessened by him. But besides this, in that chapter we referred, in passing, to the calamities of what we narrowly call 'nature,' the burnt child, the man of ruined health; and we said that these were not strictly affairs of punishment. But, undoubtedly, they are often regarded as punishment by religious men, by Christian men. We may turn to our Christian, whose best has been so good, and ask him what the mind of Christ is on this matter. Does the Lover and Father of Jesus inflict plague and pestilence, earthquake and fire, on evil-doers, as a human judge inflicts prison or the hangman's cord, and once inflicted mutilation and torture? The God of the Old Testament, so his prophets said, was not unlike our judges. What is the God of the New, as Jesus showed him? The answer is not far to seek.

'Ye have heard that it hath been said'—'But I say unto you.' He maketh his sun to rise on the evil and on the good, and sendeth rain on the just and on the unjust.' ... 'those eighteen, upon whom the tower in Siloam fell, and slew them, think ye that they were sinners above all men that dwelt in Jerusalem?' And then the warning words—'I tell you, Nay: but, except ye repent, ye shall all likewise perish.' Warning, these last words are, and, it may be, puzzling. They seem to imply punishment, doom, in this falling of a tower, though no sinners were specially selected from others for the death it brought. What is there behind this? Let us think, and bring to bear on the problem what we have learnt about the world (and therefore about God) elsewhere. And let us consult with the Christian. He is our authority now on his own affairs, as the philosopher and the scientific man are on theirs. Well, in the first place it is plain that no one of our authorities countenances arbitrary enactment. Thus much is plain about the events of nature (usually so-called), that they are no more arbitrary than the judgements, or the punishment and forgiveness, of a just man or a just God. What we want to know is the way in which their order is related to the order of justice between persons. That a tower falls on eighteen sinners who are not worse sinners than those upon whom it does not fall looks bad for justice and consequently for love. But is it bad?

We are opening up one of the most formidable of problems. Let us bear in mind, however, that we have seen one thing precluded by the mind of Christ—a belief on our part that the man who suffers or dies from an 'accident' or catastrophe of nature is thereby pointed out as punished by God. The selective, though equally natural, punishments of God are of quite another order; they single out unerringly, with the utmost subtlety and fineness, man from man. They are determined for himself by each man; he works out his own damnation as he works out his own salvation, God working with him for both. And that is why the adjustment is so accurate between the man who will not be saved and the doom that falls upon him. The calamities of earth are far too rough and ready to be God's instruments of selection. When (or if) one Grand Duke is the sole survivor of a wrecked ship and a Te Deum is sung in thankfulness to God, the mind of Christ is ignored, his plain words are ignored. 'Think ye that this Grand Duke was a man of God above all men that were on that ship?' we hear him ask. And we do not hear him say that if we all repent we shall all likewise be rescued. The kingdom of heaven is neither bought nor sold, and no repentance will purchase safety upon earth.

All this lies on the face of these illuminating words spoken from the mind of Christ. But there is more to be learnt about them and from them. We are thrown back upon the mystery of the fundamental relation between matter and spirit. And if we cannot do more, we can at least consider what experience shows us every day concerning that relation and what we find when we reflect upon it. There is that tower now. Towers may be built to stand for centuries, perhaps thousands of years. There is no indication that the fall of this particular tower was due to an earthquake, against which its strength would have been useless. We may reasonably suppose that it was not strong, that there were faults in its design, or building or material, or all three or any two. A tower well designed, well built and of good materials may, perhaps, outlast mankind upon this earth. And at least it will not fall; it will only wear away and crumble. This tower fell through the fault of sinners. Was the fault moral, or was it, as we say, merely intellectual? Was there anything of the spirit about it? And we must answer that as it was fault in a human being, a spiritual and moral person, there certainly must have been moral fault. The intellectual element is not separate from the moral.

Think—if all the men concerned in building that tower had been disinterested seekers after goodness and truth and beauty, would it have fallen as it did? What, you may say (but I am assured that you will not, if you have read thus far), what is the connexion between a love of goodness, truth and beauty, and the building of a tower? What, in fact (and this you may well ask), is the true relation between spirit and life on the one hand, and the successful use of material things on the other? Does a man use them better, that is, more successfully, because he is as God would have him be, morally and spiritually?

The narrow outlook of some religious men, and their abstraction of religion from the wide range of its concerns into the narrowness of theirs, blinds them to the wide range of goodness, of beauty, and of truth. The man who is as God would have him be (according to the mind of Christ), if he had to build a tower, would seek as he seeks salvation to find out the truth of towers, of their materials, of their design and of their building. He would not only know that this was his duty, but he would know or feel that it was his heart's desire. He would throw himself into the pursuit of this truth because he was a lover of truth. And in loving truth he would show his love of God. Therefore he would use good materials, not bad, good stone, good mortar, and he would put these together with due regard to their characters, their truth. And his love of beauty would conspire with his love of truth to bring about the strength and stability of his tower. Beauty in these things is a guarantee of truth, or rather its evidence. So closely are the three linked in the love of them and the realization of them, that we may know them to be one. They are to be distinguished, but they cannot be separated, one from another. And so those builders of our tower who should be disinterested in their worship of the three in one, would (we may well say) have set up at Siloam a tower very different from that which fell. It might have endured, like the Tower of David, to this day.

Sin, then, that is, the refusal to follow after truth, beauty and goodness, and thus after God made known to the soul, had a very real connexion with the fall of that tower. But in this respect of sin its builders were no worse than other men 'who dwelt at Jerusalem.' All these men had come short of full devotion to God as they saw God, to the light they perceived, the truth they might attain, the beauty that summoned them and the goodness that should have been theirs. Not in this regard is the fall of the tower selective. Indeed there is nothing to show that it fell upon a single one of its builders, any more than that it selected the worst of the sinners. It may have caused to 'perish' a party of mere sight-seers.

Only through that solidarity of man which links 'the crimes of each to the sorrows of all' is the fault of the builders linked with the perishing of those eighteen. And again we have testimony against any selection of the bad from the good by the calamities of earth. Not even the retribution of the kind of badness which bad building is falls, by God's determination, upon the evil-doer, through instruments of the earth. They are far too rough, these things, too indiscriminating. They do not pierce to the joints and the marrow; they hit like a blind man's bludgeon.

Yet this they assuredly are not. As the personal punishment and forgiveness of God seek and find the sinner himself in the depths of his being and to the utmost of his activity, so these things, Towers of Siloam, Armageddons, plague and pestilence, search out our corporate sin and sinfulness, reach the community of sinners in their interaction. By pain and sorrow for all, they bring to light both the sins and the shortcomings of each. Our responsibility for Armageddon extends over the devastation it has wrought, as the responsibility of those builders of the tower made the deaths of the eighteen it killed their own work. In the community of life is community of crime and suffering and all their consequences. There is an identity one with another among men, which they cannot escape. They are one body even when they are not one spirit, and every member of the body may entail disaster on the rest, as he may bring redemption. If we could not hinder life we could not help it. And therefore that word of Christ which was no doubt primarily addressed to those men of Jerusalem whose sins were inviting doom, has other points of significance we need to note. 'Unless ye repent, ye shall all likewise perish.' All—the community; likewise—through aid from the calamities and catastrophes of that outer world of things and persons with which we are so closely bound, as well as from the snares and the beguiling, the temptations and betrayal, we make for ourselves in our misuse of it.

We are one with the earth—let us remember that. And even those catastrophes of earth for which we seem to have no responsibility, storm and flood and earthquake, are not cut off from a relation with ourselves that may some day be more clear. We are but beginners in the task of entering upon our heritage of earth. And when we try to look deep into the mystery of matter and spirit what we see makes us think that they are not unlike the red and violet ends of a spectrum, which between them passes from colour to colour, but which, when our analytical stretching out is over, returns to the multiplicity in unity of white light. The Christian, by his sacramentalism and his emphasis on incarnation, confesses their kinship, as does the artist when out of three sounds he frames 'not a fourth sound, but a star,' and out of mud or marble, a vision.

We cannot penetrate this mystery; but when we recognize the solidarity of man with man, we may try to remember that it must reach beyond man, not only above him but below.

When the Christian sends us to the tower of Siloam he does us good service. If all Christians had learnt their lesson from that instead of from an older tradition and many superstitions, there would have been no need to send us. We should have known long ago what it tells of the judgements of God and the heavy responsibilities of men. And if the objection is made that the immediate application of the words of the prophet was far narrower than this to which we have carried it, our answer is that the mark of prophetic teaching is its inexhaustible richness of meaning and its proof that wisdom, of its essence, applies to life in every aspect and mode that life may display.

CHAPTER VIII

*Notre liberté, dans les mouvements mêmes par
où elle s'affirme, crée les habitudes naissantes qui
l'étoufferont si elle ne se renouvelle par un effort
constant.*
Bergson.

It is quite true that to be popular a religion must be corrupt.
The fact is noted both by its critics and enemies and by its
friends and devotees. They express their minds in different
terms but they agree. There is, however, a difference running
through their agreement, at least in many cases. The critics
who are also enemies regard the corruption not strictly as
corruption but as the clearer manifestation of the true
character religion has from the beginning. The religious man
means precisely what he says when he calls it corrupt. There
is a reality, true, beautiful, good, which men in the multitude
do not find attractive, but which may be adapted, one way or
another, overlaid, delicately or barbarously perverted, to suit
them.

Jesus Christ was not popular, nor were his principles. For a
time, no doubt, people heard him gladly. He went about
among them doing good, healing, compassionate. But when
they realized how discordant with themselves his prophetic
message really was they hounded him to death. 'Not this man
but Barabbas,' they cried. Barabbas was far more popular
than this prophet without honour in the country that should
have known him best, and did know enough of him to be
sure that he and his interests were alien from them and theirs.

It is this that stands in the gate of popularity over against an
uncorrupted Christian religion, this separation from the
people and their interests as they commonly are. The
kingdom for which Jesus lived and died, the community of
wisdom and love and self-giving, is not desired by the

societies in which narrower self-interests reign. 'Change your minds,' the prophet must always say to his people, 'repent, change your minds about everything in the world, about yourselves, and about God.'

Can we wonder that bit by bit compromise creeps in? Anything so subversive must be accommodated here and there to things as they are, for things as they are have to remain—somehow. The popular conception of right government and right morals, the popular craving for magic and for royal roads and easy-going machines, for an assured salvation or an infallible guide, permeates insensibly the religion which a poetic religious genius has revealed. The divine voice is drowned in the shouting of men who will be heard and listened to. So, whether great Rome or the little Bethel be established in popularity, the Christian religion must have been corrupted in it to meet the desires and condone the sins and errors of the people who have so disastrously been won without being transformed.

Christianity became popular. Shall we, then, look for its truth in popular presentations of it? If science were popular, should we seek its truth that way? Or do we take popular philosophy, or the view of the world or of the British Constitution presented in newspapers, as our guide to the truth of these things? Yet it seems that when a man studies the Christian religion he does just what he would regard himself as a fool for doing in regard to any other serious matter. He takes it in its established and popular or once popular guise, and then says—'this, this, is what the Christian religion is.' And if another presentation is offered him, say that of the Gospels or the great mystics, prophets, saints, who have been nurtured in the true faith, and fed by the divine wisdom of Christ, he says it is not Christianity at all, because Christianity is and must be taken as the religion of Christians in the multitude, not as the private discoveries or inventions of certain gifted or peculiar men—those saints, prophets, mystics—or even as Jesus Christ himself, living, dying, living for ever, whom Nietzsche took to be the only Christian.

If a man is more careful, he seems to himself to have been as careful as he need be when he goes to the official presentation of religion by theologians and doctors, and in the organized procedure of religious government and institutions. That, he says, must show me what Christianity really is. That is Christian orthodoxy. And, undoubtedly, if he carries his investigations far he will find there much that is more valuable and more difficult to dispose of easily, than what he finds current in the multitude. Yet here he needs more caution than he usually shows, however careful he is to distinguish between the official orthodoxy and the unofficial representation of it. He needs to learn or to recall continually the manner of life and thought everywhere in regard to life's effects and tools and products. He needs to tell himself that just as in the monsters of bygone epochs on the earth life was overwhelmed in monstrosity, and in the armoured beasts it was checked by the very instruments that seemed its best protection, so in all human organizations (and every Church, whatever else it may be, is a human organization) there is an ever-present danger to the spirit and the life they have been designed, well or ill, to serve. 'Automatism dogs our steps; the formula crystallizes the living thought that gave it birth, the idea is oppressed by the word, the spirit overwhelmed by the letter.' And if to this ever-present danger to religion there is added, as there very frequently is, the insidious influence of the worldly-world, of ambition, political intrigue, the pressure of popular demands and of a narrow but immensely powerful self-interest, the religious institution, if it persists unchanged, easily—one may dare to say inevitably—ceases to bear faithful witness to the religious life.

Again, the procedure of theologians, and above all the procedure of 'theologizers,' is open and always has been open to serious question. They are aware that their work is one of science; but as it began in a time when science had not learnt its best methods, nor the necessity of ever relating itself anew to living experience, theirs is a science very far from being what we have come to know and trust as scientific. Moreover, although it does change and move and grow, far more than most of us or of its professors see or acknowledge, it has never formally adopted change and movement and growth as in principle and fact necessary for its well-being. The theologians who claim to represent the orthodoxy of by far the great majority of Christians, those of the Church, Eastern or Western, are in the main determined to make every effort to abide in the old paths, and with more or less ingenuity accord themselves with a past supposed unchanging. That the present changes, they too often deplore, that in and by their own work the past has been changed, they seem not to know. And their own reluctance to change both disguises the fact that despite themselves they have done so, and militates against the value for other people of their change. The man who looks to them as representing the Christian religion takes them at their own estimate as in the main unchanging, and judges what they give him as being 'that which was from the beginning.' Along the Christian ages Christian theologians have changed into their own likeness the 'faith once delivered to the saints' and they have but rarely been saints.

It is to the saints and the prophets that we must look for the Christian religion, rather than to its doctors. But more than to any of these it is to the Supreme Person, Christ himself, saint and prophet above and in all others.

We have already found our advantage in this for the discussions of these pages. We have caught glimpses of the depth and range of some of the principles embodied both in the teaching and in the life of Jesus. The Gospels have brought us riches, although we have only taken grains of gold from their mine here or there. The Christian whom we are using as our authority for the time being is one who has sat at the feet of Christ and has the mind of Christ. He is one, happily, among many of all ages. And if for us he has no name, no concrete existence, nevertheless, as he is he is a witness whose testimony we can put to proof. He brings his documents, and better, he appeals to the witness in ourselves as truthseekers. He makes an appeal to which some of us at least find response within us. There are moments when what he says appears to be self-evident, so firmly rooted in us is a belief in those living facts of freedom and dependence, holiness and sin, love and its rejection, of which he speaks; so little is there, if there is anything, in what we have learnt from science and philosophy, that disputes them.

As to his documents—they too both carry and call forth their witness. We have those Gospels from different men; they speak in different voices and each with its own predilection, even prejudice, and its own colouring of thought, of knowledge or ignorance, of desire. Yet which among these writers could invent his subject? Which has succeeded in seriously defacing it? Behind them all he stands, the prophet of Nazareth, Jesus—God and man, the Christian says—and draws men to himself.

No doubt the Christian has much more to tell us than we can ask him for just now, or admit to our discussion. He has a great deal to say in defence of his institutions and his theologians, which may well be said and listened to. But it remains true that for us who are now asking, not for justification of these though ample justification there may be, but for the deepest principles of the Christian religion, it is to the mind of Christ and to him who has that mind that we must turn. Jesus built up no institution, gave no laws, announced no established plans, erected no infallible authority. He gave principles, living and spiritual principles. 'The words that I speak unto you, they are spirit and they are life.' So his great mystical interpreter hears him say. And men have indeed found response to his words in the opening out of their own life and spirit.

We seek the truth and reality of spirit and life, we who are seeking here. And in this search we find ourselves more and more at one with the Christian. The view that he and his fellows take of the Christian Church, that organization which is at least meant to foreshadow the kingdom Jesus preached, lies beyond the scope of this enquiry. All that needs to be said here is that we must not and do not foreclose an enquiry that shall include it. We stand now upon the very threshold of the kingdom; and, may be, we look with longing eyes.

CHAPTER IX

There is nothing said of man throughout all scripture
but what supposes him to stand, in nature,
under a necessity of choosing something that is
natural, either life or death, fire or water.
William Law.

So far-reaching a confession of the spiritual freedom and the
spiritual dependence of man as is shown in the principles of
Christian incarnation and atonement has never been popular.
As they passed through the popular mind incarnation was
often and widely made to seem a thunderclap from on high
and atonement a transaction of the heavenly courts. All
generations have clamoured for signs; and because none,
such as they desired, has been given they have invented signs
for themselves. The spiritual union of person with person in
a coincidence of knowledge, will, aims, and mutual love, is
at once too natural to be remarked in ordinary life and too
remote from what is remarked to focus attention. It is much
easier to think of a God disguised in manhood than of one
who has taken manhood into himself and is 'made man' by a
communication of himself to the man's own self. A king can
masquerade as a beggar—that is a simple affair; but for the
king to become a beggar and the beggar a king, the one
remaining, nevertheless, beggar and the other king, is
beyond belief by men whose belief is bounded by the
behaviour of things that can be seen and handled, and by the
logic of space. And it is much easier to think of salvation as
bargained for, or bought, or handed over, than as attained
only in the union of love and the co-operation of persons. In
this corruption of religion human freedom has too often
either been lost sight of or made a fixed character of man as
man, a mark distinguishing him from other creatures and
things. He is supposed to be free, but not to have the capacity
to grow in freedom. 'Freedom of the will,' according to this,
is like the right to a vote. It is a thing-character, ready-made,

in a man, as the right to a vote is a thing-character assured to a man of a certain age and standing. A man does not advance towards spiritual freedom and grow in it; he has it as a diamond has a degree of hardness that enables it to cut glass. It is, in fact, a natural quality, not a growing achievement of growth that still goes on. Therefore it does not need to be fostered either by the man himself or by God. And it cannot be lost. So men too often have said.

On the other hand we have seen, in our enquiry, that life in its progress from its first entrance upon earth seems to have had as its aim growth towards and in spiritual freedom. The force of life, in the channel that led to man, seems to have been directed towards securing the maximum of choice and of field of choice for him, the minimum of determination and of hindrance from without. We said that the brain is an organ of indetermination; we might have said that it is the organ of a spirit seeking its fulfilment through freedom in growth, and growth in freedom. No religion which does not show congruity with what we have learnt about life can seem to us in truth of touch with it. The popular forms of Christianity do not show this congruity. Even the officially instituted forms have, according to the manner of institutions, overlaid that truth and encumbered spiritual and moral life with tradition, habit, heritage that are become its burdens instead of its instruments of expression. Therefore we have to go to the prophet and learn of him, drink from his clear fountain of living waters. There, unquestionably, we find what we seek, religion in touch, in more than touch, with life. It is one with life, this religion given and shown us in the prophet of Nazareth.

Then and there we see that the Christian doctrines of incarnation and atonement should properly have an unmistakable connexion both with our own lives, their needs and aspirations, and with truth we have come to know through men of science. Those doctrines are, to begin with, an explicit recognition of a promise of freedom which the force of emergent life has striven for and secured, and which men are called upon to realize for themselves. That men shall fulfil their destiny more and ever more of life, it seems, must become theirs. That is, more and more of the spirit and life of God must become in very fact, not merely their own, but themselves. This the Christian speaks of as the incarnation or the extension of the incarnation of God in man. And, plainly, there is nothing in the teaching of Jesus, or in his work and person, which implies that this process is mechanical or that, being spiritual, it can be inevitable. God in the nature of things, of himself, cannot—will not, if you like, it is the same—compel union with him. Therefore men can escape their destiny of union with God by rejecting his proffer of more and greater life. They have their fate in their own hands; they may choose amiss.

Then, the Christian says, that other aspect of the love of God, which in fact is only other because we speak of it as though it were and look at it in a special point of view, his atonement or reconciliation of man with himself, comes into play. Here, too, love seeks to win love, will invites the co-operation of will, and wisdom pleads. No mechanism, no compulsion, nothing arbitrary or even commanding. 'Come unto me,' he says. And every effort love can make that man may be won is made, even to that of the agony and death of the lover that the loved one may be rescued from slavery to self, and brought into the life of love and the liberty wherewith Christ would make him free.

A deepening enslavement by sin, or a growing liberty in vital union with the Christ of God—these are the alternatives put before us in the Christian religion. And again we see life— or shall we say God?—striving to give freedom, yet with no preordained success. As in the plants and beasts life found no open way for that advance, so, although in man the way was found, men can bring it to an end merely by desiring and seeking no more than gratification of the narrow interests of a self that is bounded by self-seeking. It seems that life can be as effectually checked by this as, in a lower order, it was checked by the coating of cellulose on the vegetable cell. It is possible for a man so to imprison himself in self as to shut out God, so to build a wall about himself as to cut off from his life that fountain of living waters on which its advance and true continuance depend. He contracts into an eddy, a circling stream narrowed within set boundaries of himself. He becomes as the lower beasts, but worse than they because he is no beast.

The Christian says that when this process of cutting off and shutting out reaches completion, the man is in hell. And the language of symbol and pictorial imagination has spent itself in trying to express what that really means. Naturally, the symbolism and the painting have varied with the character of imagination at different times and in different nations. What we must tell ourselves is that they are no more than this, and that they may well both falter and fail before a horror so extreme.

The shutting-down, the extinction, of a man—for this is what it amounts to—who is capable of an indefinite advance in freedom and life, in love and wisdom and knowledge—that is, in God and fellowship—is a catastrophe with which the blotting-out of all the mighty beasts of the past is incomparable. Consider, if he were the only man? Yet is he the less what he is because he is one of millions? For one man, the Christian says, Christ would die, though it is for all men that he died. 'The very hairs of your head are numbered.'

One man in hell—think of it. One man who might have been united with God in an influx of inexhaustible new life lifting him from order to order of glory—that is what the Christian sees and what leads him, or has led him often, to describe such a loss in terms from which we shrink to-day. But if we learn to see what it is the Christian means, can we say that he goes too far? Or shall we not say that if we had at our command words fit to depict his meaning they would go even farther? No doubt we see plainly the absurdity of material fires and the religious and psychological falsity of the picture of human beings vainly desiring God, when we know that, as has been said by a great Christian, 'the sun meets not the springing bud that stretches toward him, with half that certainty, as God, the Source of all good, communicates himself to the soul that longs to partake of him.' But the fact remains that to lose life in 'the second death,' to pass out of all fellowship whether with man or God, to shrink into an ever-shrivelling creature who cares for nothing outside its ever-narrowing and concentrating self-love, is for any live, loving, healthy-minded man or woman as terrible and repulsive a fate as ever a painter or poet or theologian of old times attempted to describe.

Yet it seems reasonable enough. If we will not live we shall not live. If God, the Christian says, is permitted by us to reconcile us with himself, he will reconcile us. If we do not bar out his fountains of life they will live in us as well-springs. We are wholly dependent upon receiving more of his life, but we cannot be compelled to receive it. We may even decline freedom and lose what we had of it, employing it amiss; it is not an inalienable character stamped upon us. We have grown into enough of it to be able to refuse to have more. 'Whosoever hath, to him shall be given; and whosoever hath not, from him shall be taken away even that which he seemeth to have.'

CHAPTER X

A religion that is not founded in nature is all fiction and falsity, and as mere a nothing as an idol.
William Law.

The gain or the loss of life—this is what the Christian religion calls us to face. Will you be a slave to the life you have and in the end lose it, or at least all that makes it worth living? Or will you, in the liberty wherewith Christ makes you free, take up your heritage of more life in union with him?

There is a good deal in our experience that may be read with advantage as commentary on this challenge of religion. There are men (we have known them) who grow smaller before our eyes. We say that they are wrapped up in themselves. There are others who as plainly grow larger. Their interests expand; they take in more of the concerns of other men and, as we put it, make them their own. These, obviously, far from being wrapped up in themselves, are for ever breaking down barriers and passing beyond them. If we do not see them for some time we find them happily different. They are caring about ideas and aims and persons they were not interested in before; they have been learning; they have, in one word, grown. And those others will have shrunk. A man grows by the spiritual food on which he feeds. And if such a statement sounds remote from ordinary experience (which it is not), let us say that the more he really has the more he really is.

Now religion acknowledges this and interprets it. In the eyes of a religious man such growth means a growth in God. And he points out that it happens only where a man has sought for its own sake, not for his, what he has won. He says that the way of life is a way of disinterestedness in regard to self and interestedness in all else. And, as usual, he sends us to the Gospel for the fundamental principle underlying what experience shows. 'Whosoever will save his life shall lose it.' That is the kernel of the matter. Because love is the secret of growth in spiritual life, whether intellectual, moral or aesthetic, greed shall not procure its fruits. In the nature of things it cannot. That is why growth in 'spirit and life' seems so paradoxical. When I want food to eat I may be as greedy as I please. This will not prevent me from having it. When I want food of the spirit greed will only take me out of my true path and I shall find husks that the swine eat and Dead Sea fruit.

I cannot even discover truth or beauty or holiness, much less win them to myself, if I do not seek them for their own sake. I cannot see what another man is, and I cannot make him at one with me in a real fellowship, unless I care about him (as we say) because he is what he is, and so make his interests mine. If I use any human being as a mere instrument to serve my purpose I lose that human being, though I may keep the instrument. Men and women, like goodness and truth and beauty—and God—cannot be made mine unless I give myself to them.

'It is very hard to be a Christian.' It certainly is. The man who husbands life forfeits it, and yet life is dear. 'Die to live, the philosopher advises, as his counsel of prudence. But how is a man to lay down life from nothing more than prudence? How can a man be a prudent and careful adventurer of life? He may prudently and carefully be a merchant, but never an adventurer. And true religion has no truck with merchandise or merchants of the spirit. Its watchword is love—the love that gives, the love God is, the love royal that seeks no gain, the love of Christ.

So according to religion the way of giving is, in truth and experience, the way of gain; but if we try to follow it for gain we find ourselves altogether outside the way, not giving and therefore without gain. It is hard to be a Christian. It is exceedingly hard to love as God loves. In fact we cannot, unless God shall become man in us. He is the supreme giver and our supreme gain. Inasmuch as we love the things and persons God loves, for their own sake (which, naturally, we shall do when he dwells in our hearts and our desires), we shall win them to ourselves; whether they are, for instance, goodness, truth and beauty, or our fellow-men. And in thus and to that extent winning the objects of our love we shall unveil that reality we either call by those abstract names, or find revealed in our fellows—the reality which is God. Under those mere names God himself lies concealed. 'I am the way, the truth and the life'—I myself, he says to the men who are discovering beauty or holiness or truth, am that which you ignorantly worship. 'When saw we thee?' they still may ask. Yet they knew him when through self-giving they knew these. And names are nothing, where reality is tasted, touched and handled.

As God communicates himself or gives himself to us men, in sheer love of us, so must we communicate or give ourselves to all we seek. This is the way of that life the Christian calls eternal. No man follows it unless God be with him; but every man may follow it, and will, unless he refuses God.

What, then, is it to refuse God? The answer is always the same. It is to enclose the life of self within a prison of self-seeking, to shut outside anything that seems likely to disturb this concentrated worship, to try to drag inside anything likely to profit its narrow interests, to use things and persons as its instruments of self-guarding and self-seeking. And if self-guarding and self-seeking extend to the use of the instruments of religion, as well they may in men and women of due prudence and ambition, we have the type of Pharisee whom Jesus denounced, or the type of priest who judged him and condemned him as the enemy of God. All these are in some degree refusers of God. And a religion that panders to self-guarding and self-seeking and encourages greed or makes play with fear may be popular, but however well-established, must be corrupt. So far as this goes, life is not in it, and it does but help men to disguise from themselves their loss of life.

The incarnation of God and the atonement of man with man and with God in Christ are wrought by self-giving, that is by love. The whole process of nature is a sacrament of God's self-giving, rising to the full revelation of love. These things are one. It is profoundly true that 'a religion that is not founded in nature is all fiction and falsity, and as mere a nothing as an idol.' Yet the Christian religion, pre-eminently founded in nature though it assuredly is, has been perverted, over and over again, to be an organized means by which men falsify a nature that is capable of an utmost self-giving to man and to God. The greedy and the fearful have too often captured its organization, and the adventurer of love has been driven out. But both beyond and within those built-up walls the true religion of Christ has always lived and is lasting now. Like the ferment in the meal it is everywhere alive in those who, despite all the religious self-seeking around them, share the self-sharing of God. These have always had the alchemist's touch; they have turned dross to gold and have used it to ends of God. Like the divine powers they overrule the errors of men. But the pity is that this very fact not rarely hinders both the detection and the setting right of those errors. 'See,' men say, 'this is the nursery of saints.' And confusion of judgement goes on. It is a pragmatic test that shows the danger of pragmatic tests. Let us get back to principles, for who shall dare to say whether this or that is the nurture of saints. All things work together for their good, as all things work together for the truth-seeker's truth and for beauty in its discerner's eyes. For these, nothing is common or unclean.

CHAPTER XI

Now whence was it that a religion, so serious in
its restraints, so beautiful in its outward form and
practices, and commanding such reverence from all
that beheld it, was yet charged by Truth itself with
having inwardly such an abominable nature? It
was only for this one reason, because it was a religion
of self.
William Law.

As heaven or hell depends on the choice between self-giving
and self-seeking, so does the worship of the true God or the
false. Names may be mockeries here. The self-seeking
Christian, worshipping, as he may tell us, the God and Father
of his Lord Jesus Christ, is doing nothing of the kind. He is
worshipping that which he serves. If he could really use the
true God as a means towards the end he has at heart, that is,
make God serve him, he would do so. This, in fact, is what
he tries to do. Naturally he cannot succeed. And the God
whom he thinks he worships is fiction and an idol; it is one
who is his instrument in self-seeking, and that is a fictitious
God. 'God is a Spirit; and they that worship him must
worship him in spirit and in truth.' 'Thou shalt love the Lord
thy God with all thy heart, and with all thy soul, and with all
thy mind, and with all thy strength.' Here is the first clue to
Christian worship. And the second is 'like unto it':—'Thou
shalt love thy neighbour as thyself.' The Christian comment
on this is characteristic:—'He that loveth not his brother
whom he hath seen how can he love God whom he hath not
seen?' And the test is crucial. There is no true worship
without love, and no love of God without love of the brother-
man. So the argument works itself out and finally excludes
the consistent and impenitent self-seeker from the worship
of God.

Indeed, in the nature of life in man, this exclusion is inevitable. Unless a man makes his neighbour and that neighbour's interests his own, he necessarily excludes him from himself. In the nature of living personal beings this must be, for only in harmony do persons coincide, only by the stretching out of my interests and myself to embrace do I include. I must grow if my neighbour is to become for me 'as myself' and be loved as myself. So that love of myself which is evil when confined to interests solely mine, becomes good as it expands. So the contracting of life within my narrow boundaries is escaped, and although I still love myself I love a self that grows out and forth to the inclusion of all, even to the inclusion of God, whom then I shall love with the ardour which in the contracted self is the very torment of its hell. Only the directing of that ardour beyond the self can prevent it from being a consuming fire within the self. Therefore unless I learn to worship God (and here again words, names may mock at realities), I shall 'perish' in my own flame.

Worship is no pious luxury: it is a necessity of the spiritual life. Every man who is growing in the spirit is a worshipper of God. He may never use the name, he may be one of those who would say 'Lord, when saw we thee?' but his love is showing him the true God in his own spirit and his own truth, and, in showing him too the divine way of Love with men, commands his worship. He has discovered the marvel of self-giving, and in that discovery the marvel of the divine way he cannot but adore; his life, in fact, is adoration.

From other men this way is hidden; and a God that may command their worship must be a different God and take another way. He must declare himself in a power they can recognize, that kind of power which has kinship with the forces of men's machines and has uses like the uses of machines. This God, who may perhaps, through what seems to them worship, be made a means towards their own ends, is above all a God of an all but material power. So, may be, they cringe before him, pour out praises, make sacrifices, pay a dutiful service such as a supreme power of that kind may well call forth in the men they are. And then, if there comes among them a prophet, he pleads with them in God's name, 'I will have mercy and not sacrifice.' 'To what purpose cometh there to me incense from Sheba, and the sweet cane from a far country? Your burnt offerings are not acceptable, nor your sacrifices sweet unto me.'

Just such men as these self-seekers came to Jesus, asking for a miracle, a sign. 'An evil and adulterous generation,' he said, 'seeketh after a sign.' Why 'evil and adulterous'? Surely because in seeking a sign such as would please them they were blind to the divine truth in the presence of which they stood, and, open-eyed for their own interests, were in their hearts trafficking with a false God.

That the craving for such signs, such miracle, is always evil and adulterous can hardly be said. Yet truly it partakes, in large measure, of the nature of sin. And at best it is blindness, blindness to the true marvels of God in his manifestation through 'the things that are made' and are being made. We who have learnt of the history of earth have our souls filled with marvel, and with mystery too. It is not easy for us to see how any generation that looks for more, while it has that, can be other than evil and adulterous. But the fact is that familiarity does blind men to both marvel and mystery. If it did not, the very stones we tread under foot would proclaim their witness to God, and every moment of our own life would call forth adoration of him.

In regard to this matter there is a pressing need for the meeting of science and philosophy with religion. Science and philosophy tear away the veil with which familiarity hides from us the mysteriousness and marvel of all things and of our own personal and common life. They show us unfathomed depths for wonder where we had seen nothing but a smooth accustomed surface. But it is religion that shows us God in all those depths, God made known even by the very surface, and turns our wonder into worship. It is science and philosophy that shall purge religion of the taint it has derived from both the ignorant, and the evil and adulterous, generations after generations who have made it seem what it seems. I say 'seem what it seems,' for this is not what it is. That is no true religion, certainly no religion after the mind of Christ, which passes over the marvels of the lily of the field and of the man indwelt by God and one with God, taking them as things that are of course; while making much of signs interpreted as 'intervention' and therefore taken as the only signs of a God who is nowhere and nothing to us unless he intervenes.

We stand amazed, we who have learnt now to see God everywhere. Can any religious man open his eyes, we ask, and not see signs of God? Can he search in any human life without finding signs in abundance there, signs of the life-giving presence or of the dreadful death-dealing absence of God? What more can he ask or desire? 'Lord God of hosts,' we exclaim, 'heaven and earth are full of thy glory!'

Then we turn to history, the long history of man, and the long history of the Christian religion which goes back, beyond the sublime figure who proclaimed it in Palestine, to the beginnings of the worship of God. We discover those beginnings in the first men who turned their eyes from self to the brother. We look along the ages and cease to be surprised. In his long-drawn education man has but slowly learnt to find God in more and more of his own life and the world. Step by step he has felt his way, led by the spirit given him, to the knowledge of the God and Father of Jesus Christ, the incarnate and redeeming God of all men, the God who comes to indwell all things. Only now, in a new fulness of time, are the teaching of Jesus and the revelation of his life and death finding a new context in new knowledge and reflective thought. Only now are we beginning to see why, if knowledge and reflective thought have so far done their work, it may well be an evil and adulterous generation that seeks for any other signs than those which they and Christ reveal. Just what the earthly presence of the God-revealing Jesus was to that generation—a test of their single-mindedness and will to receive and welcome divine truth— so, when his life and witness meet with a new emphasis in the less but concurrent witness of new knowledge, this generation of religious men is put to the same test. Will they receive new witness to his truth and to God? or will they reject it because it has no likeness to those signs that to their minds are alone fitted to show God? Will they or will they not have humility enough to learn of scientific and philosophic 'builders of Jerusalem' concerning the true methods of God?

We cannot tell; that is, of this generation. But we may trust in the prevailing strength of truth. Generations pass, but that endures. And the prophet's word goes on:—'the hour cometh, and now is, when the true worshippers shall worship the Father in spirit and in truth.'

CHAPTER XII

Nel suo profondo vidi che s'interna,
legato con amore in un volume,
cio che per l'universo si squaderna.
Dante.

For the Christian the barrier that finally checks the advance
of life is not death but a self-concentrated self. It is freedom
misused and lost, freedom turning against the life that has
striven to bring it to birth. Perversity builds that barrier and
human life cannot pass it or—shall we not say with the
Christian?—God cannot pass it. This alone thwarts the
divine purpose for man and brings about the 'second' and
only true death.

We have nothing to urge against this teaching of religion; we
see the second death beginning in every man who is
perverting freedom from its life-furthering office. We see in
him that which he seems to have being taken away.
Moreover, we are prepared to believe that the first death,
willingly accepted (as we have also seen) as an element in
purposive and potent life, is but the gate through which men
pass to more of life. We may have our moments of doubt,
because we cannot see with our eyes the other side of that
gate, and the sense-habit is strong within us; but reason
demands, as the Christian religion declares, that life that is
growing here and is big with promise unfulfilled shall go on
there.

The Christian seems to know much of the other side of that
gate that other people do not know. He talks of heaven, of
paradise, of hell. We understand him when he talks of hell;
there is so much evidence of that here and now. But we are
less clear about his paradise, less clear still about his heaven.
What does he really mean when he speaks, all too positively
and definitely (we think), about these two?

Undoubtedly most Christians have meant a good many things at which not a few of them will smile now. They have meant things that were certainly not of the mind of Christ, but of the unilluminated and uncriticizing and biased minds of other men. Sometimes they have pictured a man who is, even to our eyes, a mere beginner in the divine art of life, plunged, as it were, into a very sea of God, sent with all his mere beginnings to live as he may amid God's unveiled glories. That is not a picture which instructed and enlightened Christians favour now. Our friend to whom we so constantly appeal will tell us of Paradise, where Jesus and the thief were to meet together. He will speak of 'intermediate' purifying and enriching states through which the beginner passes, learning his art of life. He will assure us that he knows of very few who even to his poor vision seem fit to 'go to heaven,' fit, that is, to endure the full glory of beauty and holiness and truth resplendent and realized in the 'beatific vision' of God. And in this he commends himself. He is an evolutionist of the coming worlds, this believer in an advance through them towards the splendours of the City of God. And after all he has the collective voice of Christendom speaking with him. Only a minority of Christians from the beginning until now have not been evolutionists of the worlds to come.

No doubt the Christian arranges his pictorial conceptions of those worlds too systematically, and marks off grades as life never does. But in the main life has kept its hold upon him and he has been unable not to see that it must go on, move, change, grow, on the far side of death. We have no quarrel with his principle in this regard, though we may contest the mechanical fashion in which, not rarely, he applies it. And when he speaks of the 'beatific vision' of the City of God, our hearts are stirred in response. We too seek a 'continuing city' of life in its grandeur. We, too, see the promise of that city here, even in the very failures of our own. And when the

Christian tells us of his Lord's Prayer—Thy kingdom come, as it is in heaven, we feel that heaven is not alien from us or from our desires and our hopes. If heaven is indeed the crown and consummation of personal and social life on earth, then it is to heaven we ourselves are looking forward, looking, fearing, longing. We, too, have our vision of a kingdom where love shall be the king, and self-seeking, with all its dreadful consequences, be done away. We can see it is this that ruins our cities of earth, this alone. And where this is not, there indeed will be our kingdom come, as well as God's.

An Eastern's imagination may depict the 'holy city, the new Jerusalem,' in her 'light,' as 'pure gold, like unto clear glass'; he may exhaust that imagination in details of chalcedony and emerald and pearl; that is his way. But when he says that 'the nations of them which are saved shall walk in the light of it: and the kings of the earth do bring their glory and honour into it,' he gives speech to our mind through his. For this, this, is the 'goal of human endeavour' for us. We have watched the advance of life towards our own cities and in turn watching them have discovered what they lack and what, in their poverty of attainment and abundant promise, they foretell if life goes on beyond the gates of death. So, sharing the Christian's faith that indeed it does, we share his vision.

Only as a social being is any man a man at all. Only when the promise of other men is fulfilled, is his promise fulfilled. No man (we see that plainly) can be 'saved' alone; he must be saved in his nations, by true community in a life grown to be harmonious with life everywhere, in and with the source of all life. Only in God can any man fulfil his destiny as a man among men who must be one with them if he is not to 'perish everlastingly.' We and the Christian agree—once we see what he means and he sees what we mean. And it is through Jesus Christ that we discover the meaning of the Christian. We may, perhaps, not unsuitably, urge him to try to discover ours in the same way. For it is only when he has wandered from the side of Christ and forgotten or misinterpreted the mind of Christ that there is trouble between us.

It is easy to forget and misinterpret, very easy to substitute for divine spirit and life and the divine 'word,' a machinery of logic or tradition or institutional arrangement. But it is destructive of the possibility of mutual understanding between us. Again, we must urge, it is machine-like scheming that divides, not real religion or knowledge of life. 'Ye have made the word of God of none effect through your tradition' is a prophet's saying of the widest application in the affairs of men. But when we recognize this, even on one side only of a dividing line, the process of correction has begun. And as a matter of fact there is recognition now on both sides, and day by day it extends itself and its influence. Science and philosophy and religion are met together as they have never in the history of the world been met before, open-eyed, conscious of the common heritage of training in the battle of the world and in the struggles of practical life, which has biased every one of us and been the chief agent in turning the common search after truth by men of good will into a war of opinions.

To confess that we are all, in so far as we are honest seekers, 'builders of Jerusalem' after our own manner and degree, is the first and perhaps the hardest step to take towards full co-operation between us. What children we are, that we do not know it! Yet, in truth, we cannot know it until on both sides we give up the fond belief, the delusion, that we are not seekers but have either attained or received, either attained the full truth of the world and ourselves by knowledge, or received it through an external and externally given revelation. Once we know that we are all pilgrims and that the divine city lies ahead for every one of us, both in knowledge and in life, we may travel together.

With the Christian we may work for the divine kingdom. We share his belief and his trust in the omnipotence of redeeming love. Nothing, we see, can redeem this earth but love. There is love to be seen faintly, amid dark and conflicting shadows, in the biologist's picture of a world-Eden, where it is after all and in spite of all 'creation's final law.' But the fulness of its glory is unveiled only in the love of Christ, passing our knowledge.

'Conceiving our life in this manner, the material evolution of the world becomes the incarnation and the expression of a spiritual meaning, of a divine event which is actually in process of coming to pass. No longer, for example, do we think of the earth's movement round the sun as a meaningless rotation: we think of it as preparing the conditions which enable life to rise to its sublimest height, we see the whole creation saturated in sunlight. Not in vain are the heavens starred with innumerable fires. They speak to us of worlds to which they give life and being, warming them with their heat, brightening them with their beams. And the end to which all these lives are moving, of every flower that blooms, of every bird that sings, is also the central principle of the entire evolution of the universe—the embodied Word of God. For the purpose of the whole is nothing other than the incarnation of the divine, the participation of the created in the eternal life of the uncreated, of which the God-man is the perfect revelation.... If God be indeed the end of all existence, he must needs fill all things with his being. If God is love, his arms are round the entire universe, and there is no creature anywhere unloved by him.'

Prince Eugene Troubetzkoy.

www.ingramcontent.com/pod-product-compliance
Lightning Source LLC
LaVergne TN
LVHW051643080426
835511LV00016B/2468

* 9 7 8 1 6 3 9 2 3 2 0 8 6 *